BARBARA A. GREENE

Self-Efficacy and Future Goals in Education

NEW YORK AND LONDON

First published 2018
by Routledge
711 Third Avenue, New York, NY 10017

and by Routledge
2 Park Square, Milton Park, Abingdon, Oxon, OX14 4RN

Routledge is an imprint of the Taylor & Francis Group, an informa business

© 2018 Taylor & Francis

The right of Barbara Greene to be identified as author of this work has been asserted by her in accordance with sections 77 and 78 of the Copyright, Designs and Patents Act 1988.

All rights reserved. No part of this book may be reprinted or reproduced or utilised in any form or by any electronic, mechanical, or other means, now known or hereafter invented, including photocopying and recording, or in any information storage or retrieval system, without permission in writing from the publishers.

Trademark notice: Product or corporate names may be trademarks or registered trademarks, and are used only for identification and explanation without intent to infringe.

Library of Congress Cataloging-in-Publication Data
A catalog record has been requested for this book

ISBN: 978-1-138-69692-1 (hbk)
ISBN: 978-1-138-69691-4 (pbk)
ISBN: 978-1-315-52301-9 (ebk)

Typeset in Joanna MT
by Apex CoVantage, LLC

Self-Efficacy and Future Goals in Education

As the inner resource that drives us to pursue activities, to put forth effort, and to avoid failure, motivation is key to overall well-being. Self-efficacy and future goals are important to understanding and reinforcing the motivation to learn, especially for students in classroom settings. Written by a leading expert on motivation, this book situates the topic within the broader context of educational psychology research and theory, and brings it to a wider audience. With chapters on the fundamentals of self-efficacy and future goals, their importance for student learning, and how to develop them in educational settings, this concise volume is designed for any education course that includes student motivation in the curriculum. It will be indispensable for student researchers and both pre- and in-service teachers alike.

Barbara A. Greene is a Brian E. and Sandra O'Brien Presidential Professor of Educational Psychology at the University of Oklahoma, USA.

Ed Psych Insights
Series Editor: Patricia A. Alexander

Assessment of Student Achievement
Gavin T. L. Brown

Self-Efficacy and Future Goals in Education
Barbara A. Greene

Self-Regulation in Education
Jeffrey A. Greene

Strategic Processing in Education
Daniel L. Dinsmore

Cognition in Education
Matthew T. McCrudden and Danielle S. McNamara

Emotions at School
Reinhard Pekrun, Krista R. Muis, Anne C. Frenzel, and Thomas Goetz

Teacher Expectations in Education
Christine Rubie-Davies

Classroom Discussions in Education
Edited by P. Karen Murphy

Contents

One:	**Introduction**	**1**
Two:	**Theoretical Underpinnings**	**10**
Three:	**Self-Efficacy**	**33**
Four:	**Future Goals**	**50**
Five:	**Implications for Motivating Others**	**63**
Six:	**Conclusions**	**82**

Glossary	87
References	90
Index	97

One
Introduction

Understanding human motivation is one of the major concerns across disciplines such as philosophy, religion, politics, marketing, and education. Motivation is the inner resource that drives us to pursue activities, to put forth effort, and to avoid failure. Motivation to learn, or academic motivation, is particularly important due to the amount of time people spend in school and the perception that many students seem unmotivated to learn in school; its links to achievement and positive health outcomes; and strong arguments made by researchers, such as Ryan and Deci,[1] that motivation is key to overall well-being. However, there are many facets of motivation, including intrinsic versus extrinsic, outcome expectations, self-efficacy, values, and goals. In this book, the focus will be on two concepts related to motivation: self-efficacy and future goals.

Self-efficacy is a person's belief about whether s/he is capable of successfully completing a given task. The task might be learning a new skill, baking a good cake, or earning a high grade on an exam. By future goals, I am referring to goals that are personally meaningful and that guide people through school and other efforts. The goals may be relatively close in time, such as the goal of passing a class, or they may be more distant, such as the goal of graduating college or becoming a successful app developer. The main thesis of this book is that self-efficacy and future goals are critical to understanding and supporting motivation to learn, especially the motivation to learn in classroom settings. In order to grasp why these concepts are important, we need to first examine other motivational concepts.

THE DISTINCTION BETWEEN EXTRINSIC AND INTRINSIC MOTIVATION

There are several common ways in which people conceptualize motivation. For example, we often think about rewards and punishment, which are aspects of extrinsic motivation. We know from everyday experience that fear of punishment can guide our behavior (i.e., we are motivated to avoid punishment). We also know that rewards can encourage us to repeat behaviors that previously resulted in achieving a reward, such as getting a good grade to receive praise from parents. This illuminates an important characteristic of motivation in general; it governs the activities that we avoid and approach. Motivation guides the direction of people's energy. Rewards and punishments are extrinsic, in that they are not inherent in the task or behavior, but rather external to it. We know, again from everyday experience, that they can be motivating, but evidence tells us that they do not help us understand ongoing motivation or motivation over time.[1,2,3] Additionally, when their actions are largely governed by rewards and punishments, people are less likely to believe that they are in control of their lives and less likely to experience positive emotions such as enjoyment, hope, and curiosity.

Since feelings of control and emotional well-being are important to humans, rewards and punishment do not sustain motivation. The evidence demonstrates that people who have largely externalized motivation will go through motions of whatever the behavior is, but are less likely to embrace the task meaningfully. Think of the fifth-grade student who does not enjoy reading and feels like it is just a struggle without fun or reason. She does the reading-related assignments enough to keep out of trouble with the teacher, but is not invested in learning to read better or gaining new knowledge from reading. Instead, she just goes through the lessons without much thought. In order for people like this student to fully engage and benefit from learning, there needs to be more internalized purpose or meaning found in the task. Many people seek other parts of their lives for more positive motivation. It may be that her family life is meaningful or she has a hobby that allows her to feel energetic and happy.

Implicit in the discussion of rewards and punishment is the need for more internalized meaning to energize motivated activity. The most internalized form of motivation is intrinsic motivation.[1] When people are enjoying the task at hand, they are intrinsically motivated to complete that task. When we experience this type of motivation, we are devoted to and engaged fully in the task. We work hard, but do not feel like we are working hard. We pursue the task repeatedly, and as a result, we keep getting better at it. Think if the fifth-grade student who is still struggling with reading finds a genre that she loves. Perhaps she discovers graphic novels and realizes that reading is enjoyable and interesting. She now might engage in reading for an hour or so a day. This will help her develop her reading skills so that she will become more proficient, thereby making most of her schoolwork less of a struggle. Clearly, intrinsic motivation is the gold standard of motivation—it is completely internalized and creates positive emotions. The problem is that much of life, for most people, is not filled with intrinsically rewarding tasks. If we only worked hard when intrinsically motivated, we would likely not become proficient at all the school subjects that we need to master—at least to some degree.

Many people agree that young children come to school intrinsically motivated to learn. As we move from pre-K settings, schools and classrooms become less child-focused (that is, focused on stimulating the interests of the child) and more reward-governed. Most students are shaped by those strong cues in the environment. Teachers need to be aware of the fact that it is the current nature of schooling and classrooms that undermines students' intrinsic motivation. Teachers, though, can structure their classrooms in ways that mitigate against the undermining of student motivation.[2,3] One way in which they can do this is to understand how motivation can be maintained when learning involves repetition and other forms of inherently uninteresting practice for learning new skills.

SUSTAINED EFFORT DEPENDS ON MOTIVATION

Let us consider the task of learning to play guitar as one example before we explore a classroom example. Most people choose to learn an instrument because they assume that they will enjoy the resulting skill. However, it takes many hours of boring practice to develop the skill that might result in intrinsic motivation. An important question: How do we motivate someone, or our self, to engage in the degree of practice that will result in skill development? There is no one answer to that question because different motivations will work for different people, but understanding the potential roles of self-efficacy and future goals will provide a framework for thinking about possible solutions. First, I need to believe that I am capable of learning the guitar, or there is no way I will invest the time in trying. That is why most music programs start people off with easy songs that a novice can learn. Learning easy songs shows the guitar student that she can be successful thereby building up her self-efficacy for learning. Additionally, after mastering a few easy songs, I can now imagine myself playing the music I want to learn. Mastery experiences, as in those times when I have been successful, provide the strongest evidence to support self-efficacy.[4]

Now, if I only have Andrés Segovia or Jimi Hendrix as the models for my future guitar playing, I am likely to give up because it will take so long to get even close to that level of expertise. I am likely to be discouraged before I get too far. But when I am able to learn some easier songs, I can use those songs as motivation to learn more complex songs. Mastery of easy songs provides me with the self-efficacy to continue trying to learn more difficult songs, and I can set goals for my future playing that include learning more difficult songs. That is why most guitar teaching programs have students learn songs right away using simplified versions of popular songs or fun songs that are easy to learn. Being able to play songs right away provides evidence that one can continue being successful in learning.

However, if I start with difficult songs, it may take too long for me to be able to play and my motivation may not be sustained. The reason is that I will need to play the different segments of a song, over and over again, before it even sounds like a song. I will need to practice both left and right hand techniques, over and over again, before those hands will be able to produce recognizable music. I will need evidence that this practice is paying off or I am likely to give up. Most meaningful complex learning has some element of boring and challenging practice that is required before the student can truly enjoy the fruits of learning. We need to help students see the reason for keeping at it, when the challenge and boredom seem more obvious to the student than the meaning behind the learning or the enjoyment that they expect to experience at some future time.

Now let's use learning algebra as another example. Although some students might begin their algebra class with intrinsic motivation, others will not, since the newness of the problems often makes the challenge more overt than the anticipated fun. Students who master algebra in the first course may go on to experience intrinsic motivation for solving algebra problems. Sadly, there are not many students who get to this point in motivation for mathematics. The evidence actually suggests that intrinsic motivation for mathematics goes down during the secondary years.[5] Even if self-efficacy for mathematics is high for certain students in elementary school, it may not be sustained for learning algebra since students cannot recognize their past mastery experiences when faced with problems that look different and more complex. That lack of efficacy, then, is complicated by students not knowing why algebra is important. Often students are not able to see the future utility of algebra. Of course, good teachers who are able to help students build their self-efficacy in this new form of mathematics show them why learning algebra is meaningful. Unfortunately, many students are not able to find the motivation that will allow them the experience of mastering algebra. As a result, they will never experience intrinsic motivation for higher-level mathematics. In fact, they may never develop the level of mathematical understanding to excel in a variety of academic subjects or to pursue a career they might have otherwise sought. I argue that if we can understand self-efficacy and future goals, we will have powerful tools to use in building students' motivation to learn.

CLASSROOMS VERSUS INDIVIDUALS

As we consider the importance of self-efficacy and future goals in motivation for learning, we need to think about both classroom issues and individual issues. Motivation resides within individuals, and teachers often need to figure out why certain individuals are not engaged in learning. That is why it is important to look at examples of individuals with motivational challenges—like we all experience when learning something new or something that is beyond our current comfort zone. However, we also want to think about implications for classrooms overall.

Classroom-level implications are concerned with how the overall environment of the classroom can support intrinsic motivation, student self-efficacy, and future goals. Nurturing students' interests in the classroom is central to intrinsic motivation.[2,3] In order to do that, teachers need to identify students' interests, build those interests into lessons, and then avoid distracting students with external rewards. There are other aspects of the classroom climate that can address self-efficacy and future goals directly. For example, research has shown that lessons that pose moderate challenges to students are optimal for positive self-efficacy.[3] Lessons that are too easy or too difficult do not support students' needs (as we will discuss in the next chapter). This also means that there should be some differentiation among students in regards to the specific tasks they are assigned to complete for a lesson. Such differentiation helps students focus on their own goals rather than comparing themselves to others. To support future goals through classroom practice, teachers can introduce lessons with a pitch for why they are relevant to students. Teachers should explain lessons in terms of how the material can be useful (i.e., for everyday life or future goals) so that students who are not intrinsically interested will still see personal relevance in the classroom activity. Some of these ideas will be discussed throughout the book.

CONCLUSION

If we want to encourage students to do well in school, and to do well with learning in general, then we need more motivational tools than either rewards and punishment or the promise/hope of intrinsic motivation. Students need to feel efficacious enough to try to learn in different subjects and they need to have reasons for trying when they are not intrinsically motivated. There are many practices that teachers can use to offset the general trend of school undermining motivation to learn. The remainder of this book will explain and support the thesis that focusing on student self-efficacy and future goals can offer powerful tools. We will examine scenarios that involve individuals and classrooms.

In developing the ideas for this book, I have chosen two examples of individuals to stream throughout. One will be a student of guitar whose experiences derive from my own but are also somewhat contrived to make particular points. There will also be an example of a seventh-grade girl recommended for eighth-grade algebra. I will use these examples because, often, when we need to apply motivation concepts, we do so in response to the challenges of individuals in our classrooms and lives. However, I will also present classroom-level applications. This would be the larger lens through which a teacher would look when considering how s/he is supporting or not supporting the self-efficacy and future goals within his/her classroom. These scenarios will also have a strong basis in observation of real classrooms, but I will embellish them for emphasis.

In the next chapter, I will summarize the two "big" theories that are most important for situating these two concepts (self-efficacy and future goals) within the larger literatures. The concept of self-efficacy came out of Social Cognitive Theory, which was developed to capture how humans use both environmental information and internal thoughts to govern their behaviors. Self-Determination Theory is a meta-theory that describes the importance of feeling in control of one's life for positive ongoing motivation.[1,6]

The third chapter focuses on defining and supporting the importance of self-efficacy for motivation for learning. The fourth chapter then focuses on future goals and why I chose to present these rather than other goals. In the fifth chapter, I present implications for our individual example students and for classrooms. Finally, in the sixth chapter, I present conclusions, caveats to my arguments, and some ideas about where the research needs to go for further application to practice.

Two
Theoretical Underpinnings

The purpose of this chapter is to summarize the two big theories from which the constructs of self-efficacy and future goals derive. Although people sometimes criticize theories for not providing actionable implications, theories can be very useful for understanding many aspects of human thought and behavior. Theories help us make predictions and allow us to test predictions within frameworks that help us explain why people feel and act certain ways while attempting to learn. Without a theoretical framework, schools often fall into the trap of trial and error or they grasp pop psychology ideas (e.g., classifying people as left-brain versus right-brain) that rarely provide positive effects or enduring changes. The benefit of using a theory is that you have a blueprint for trying out ideas; the evidence that comes out of those "experiments" then feeds back to the theory, so that the theory can grow and be modified. For this book, Bandura's Social Cognitive Theory and Self-Determination Theory will be the guiding theories.[1,6]

Before presenting these theories, I would like to provide some explanation of how theories like the two discussed in this chapter are generally tested. Because this book is focused on motivation to learn and academic success, most of the research that I am using to make my claims about self-efficacy and future goals involves trying to explain why students

Theoretical Underpinnings 11

succeed or fail in different achievement settings. It is very hard to manipulate motivation variables, as in experimental research, so we often have correlation studies rather than experimental tests of interventions, though I will mention some of these. Often, we have multiple measures of the concepts of interest, self-efficacy, and other motivation measures, then some outcome measure related to achievement that we measure with a given sample in an achievement setting. We then test the degree to which the measures are related to each other and whether or not some of the measures can statistically explain the outcome measure. Importantly, a single study tells us very little because that one study might be a fluke. Instead, we look at findings across a number of studies before we can confidently support some relationship between and among variables. My hope is that having this small amount of background on how theories are tested might help with understanding some of the findings that I will review in support of the importance of self-efficacy and future goals.

SOCIAL COGNITIVE THEORY

Social Cognitive Theory (SCT) was designed to explain how people are influenced to act or behave. SCT holds that thought, behavior, and contextual information work in reciprocal ways to guide the motivations and actions of people.[6] The theory combines elements of behaviorism (the role of reinforcement and punishment), cognitive theory, and the role of the social context to explain human functioning. It is considered a big theory because it encompasses a wide spectrum of experience and it spawns smaller theories, such as self-efficacy theory.[6] I will add some brief historical information to situate SCT in the history of psychology.

Moving Away From Behaviorism

For many years (from about the 1920s through the 1950s), psychology was dominated by the behaviorist view that all behaviors were best understood by the concepts of reinforcement and punishment.[3,7,8] During this period, many psychologists thought that studying the mind was irrelevant since behavior was overt and therefore straightforward to analyze. Any behaviors reinforced, they believed, would increase or be maintained. Praise, compliments, and other forms of external rewards were thought to be effective in reinforcing desired learning behaviors. Punishments were used to stop or decrease behaviors, while the withholding of reinforcements or extinction was the less dramatic or less forceful way to discourage unwanted behaviors. However, behaviorism was found to be an inadequate theory for explaining how people become so flexible in their use of language and complex decision-making. These concerns, and others, stimulated what has been called the "cognitive revolution."[8] The cognitive revolution was a refocus on how conscious and unconscious mental activity could be studied and used to theorize about how information from the environment is processed for learning, behaving, and overall human thriving. There were other factors that lead to the cognitive revolution, including the use of computers to record precise measurements, but the main point here is that by the 1950s, psychology was ready to move beyond its singular focus on overt behaviors to include the study of the inner processing of experience.

Thought Influences Behavior

One of the benefits of behaviorism is that it explains how contextual cues, or information in the environment, shape how people behave. If our guitar student is laughed at for

Theoretical Underpinnings 13

trying to play with the style and proficiency of Jimi Hendrix, she might be discouraged from playing that type of music. Similarly, when teachers rely on saying "No" or "Wrong," their students are less likely to raise their hands to speak in class. Human behavior clearly does respond to positive and negative consequences. However, humans also use thoughts to determine behavior. In fact, we have cognitions (thoughts) before and after we behave. Those thoughts include making sense of the social environment and understanding ourselves and our needs. SCT incorporates all three facets of human agency: personal cognitions, behaviors, and the social context. SCT is different from behaviorism because the theory holds that learning does not need to involve overt behavior. In addition, a central aspect of SCT is the notion of the self as a system that engages in forethought, self-reflection, and symbolic functions (such as language) to understand and negotiate life.[6] So, while behaviorism held that external consequences were the main motivators of human action, SCT holds that people are motivated to action based on both external and internal information interpreted by the self-system.

In SCT there are three components that interact with and influence one another. They are personal characteristics (including thoughts, feelings, and motivations), behavior (and consequences of past behaviors), and the environment and all the information therein. Bandura calls this interaction "triadic reciprocality"[6] (p. 23). There are three aspects to a person's experience that influence him/her in reciprocal ways. We think and feel and we look to cues in the environment (or context/situation) for what those thoughts and feelings might mean, all of which influences our behavior. Our actions make changes to the environment, as people respond to what we do, and then we reflect on both the behavior and the response, which again influences our behavior. For example, when children come to the United States from countries where schooling is more formal, they might feel anxious and confused when they first encounter a school environment that looks and feels different from those in their country of origin. When the teacher and other students are welcoming and friendly, this signals to the children that they can relax. If the new students smile and act friendly in response, then the friendliness is encouraged. However, if the new students are too scared to smile and look at others, then the response from the US children might be to cease outward displays of friendship. Thus, there are reciprocal influences at work.

From everyday experience, we can see that people are not equally adept at using environmental cues. Some children are seemingly unaware of how others respond to their actions and how the environment cues certain behaviors. These children will be especially lost if the cues for appropriate classroom behaviors are ambiguous or understated. That is one reason why classroom structures are so important. I will say more about that later. For now, let me illustrate this notion of the triadic influences by noting that what we call impulsive behavior is when children (or adults) engage in actions without utilizing the environmental cues or their own powers of forethought and reflection.

According to Bandura, people learn due to the interaction of symbolic, vicarious, and self-regulatory processes.[6] Symbolic processes refer to our abilities to use language, concepts, and other abstract ideas to think about our world and communicate those thoughts to others. A major limitation with behaviorist views of learning was that there was no accounting for the role of symbolic processing, even though language use is a major component of human functioning. Related to

Theoretical Underpinnings 15

that form of processing, we watch how others fare in our different social environments and use that vicarious experience to form ideas about our own experiences. This is the crux of social learning; we learn through observations of others. We symbolize those observations in our thoughts so that we can make sense out of the experiences of others for ourselves. Finally, in making sense out of our thoughts, we can use self-regulatory processes to steer and correct our behaviors. Both SCT and SDT recognize human agency, or control over one's own life, as the centerpiece of learning and motivation. Such control requires self-regulation.

Self-regulation describes how people go about governing their own lives, especially as they seek to achieve important goals. (It is, by no accident, the central topic of another book in this series.)[9] Self-regulation involves setting goals, organizing activities to meet those goals, monitoring progress, and reacting to the progress—or lack thereof—with rewards and punishments. In SCT, the thoughts that occur in response to the environment and prior experiences are used to help people self-regulate, or make decisions about whether their current path is working out or needs to be modified. For example, a student from another country who is too nervous to act friendly on his first day in school in the United States might reflect on his goal to be liked and to have friends and how that first experience did not help him achieve that goal. He could change his behavior the following school day in the hope of making better progress toward that goal than what he accomplished the first day. Of course, some people are better at self-regulation than others, and we are not completely self-regulated in all aspects of our lives. For example, a student might be more self-regulated with regard to her guitar playing than with her schoolwork. However, we can

Theoretical Underpinnings

and should encourage students toward greater self-regulation in their lives.

There are two important findings from research on self-regulation: 1) People are more successful at achieving goals when they are more self-regulated in trying to achieve those goals; and 2) People are more self-regulated when they have positive thoughts, feelings, and motivations in a given context.[10] Teachers and parents who want to see students achieve their goals need to consider whether students recognize their ability to exert control over their schoolwork, their social lives, and in their athletic or other extracurricular pursuits. We need to make sure they know how to engage in self-regulation. Like other important skills, we often need to teach students the component skills of self-regulation. We can teach them how to set goals and different ways to make progress toward goals. We can show them systems for tracking progress. Finally, we can teach them strategies for encouraging their own progress. However, unless students recognize their agency, they are unlikely to become self-regulated. One common example is students who believe they are "just not good at math." These students see math as an ability that they do not possess and, therefore, they do not recognize their agency in learning math. We can see the roles of interaction and reciprocality that Bandura suggested in SCT. Our thoughts, behaviors, and the social context work together—in complex ways—to guide us through life.

Let us consider an example of a middle school student learning algebra for the first time. Jenice is a seventh-grade girl who has been recommended for eighth-grade algebra. Her mother is a civil engineer and her father is a visual artist, and they both encourage Jenice to follow her interests and talents. While her home environment is neutral to somewhat positive about her taking the eighth-grade math, her school environment may be less supportive if she does not know anyone else who is taking eighth-grade math. Let's assume that, based on her observations at school, she understands that most seventh-grade students do not take eighth-grade math and that there are no seventh-grade girls in that class. These observations can lead her to worry about being teased for being a "smarty pants," which would be very unpleasant, especially now that she has a nice set of friends at that school. We can imagine the cognitions that she will have in response to the different cues in the environment. Some students would decline the offer given the murky evidence that it might work out. Other students would seek further evidence and perhaps wait to see how it goes. Jenice would need to weigh the evidence in light of what goals are most important to her. SCT would suggest that if Jenice could see another student who enjoys the algebra class, and is successful, and who is seen as similar to Jenice, the other student would provide some vicarious encouragement for Jenice to try the class by modeling that enjoyment and success. Therefore, SCT allows us to understand motivation and learning by making predictions based on the student's thoughts, the context, and her behaviors in the context. Next, we will move our lens to the classroom level.

Implications of SCT for the Classroom

SCT can explain much of what we see happening in classrooms. Students use situational information to inform how they act and assess what the classroom holds for them personally. At many levels of schooling, peers provide stronger cues for behavior than do other structures in the classroom (such as rewards and punishments offered by the teacher). When a majority of students are visibly engaged in a lesson, then the situation signals to all students that engagement is the appropriate behavior. Many classroom management problems occur when students do not have internalized motivations for learning and there are not enough cues in the classroom to signal positive behavior.

A good way to explore how SCT works in classrooms can be through descriptions of different classrooms and the nature of children's behavior in those different classroom settings. Some teachers provide a wealth of cues to signal what they want students to do in their classrooms. They post rules and discuss with students the nature of those rules. They post motivational posters about famous people who did well in school. They display student work to show what the class has been working on over a particular grading period. They arrange their rooms to provide spaces for library research and computer-based work. These teachers typically designate other places for students to turn in work for grading and to pick up new assignments. In other words, they arrange their classrooms to present students with unambiguous information about what they should be doing so that the teacher does not need to spend time every day prescribing actions. Instead, students are able to work independently or in groups, depending on the nature of the lesson. If there is a new student in the class, another student can easily explain how the class works during routine days.

Then there are other teachers who do not use the classroom space to signal expectations to students. Sometimes these teachers have simply kept the décor from a previous teacher. There may be rules on the walls, but those rules have not been explained or even referred to. Routines evolve for each separate class (assuming this is a secondary classroom)

Theoretical Underpinnings 19

rather than being planned in advance. In this environment, the student needs to use more of his/her cognitive resources to infer their actions and behavior. They will need more verbal information from the teacher each day before they can begin work. There are many secondary teachers who can have this type of relaxed atmosphere and still have optimal time spent on learning. These teachers need to take more care to ensure that students are on task and that discipline is used consistently. Without explicitly expressed expectations (such as classroom rules), the teacher can fall into the trap of calling out students for misbehavior in an inconsistent manner, perhaps influenced more by the teacher's mood than by student conduct. Rules and other cues in the environment, then, can provide structure to classrooms to encourage positive or on-task learning behaviors in students.

We should also note, however, that effective secondary teachers sometimes rely more on the social environment than on physical space to provide information about learning and motivation in their classrooms. These teachers find ways to demonstrate care and respect for students as well as consistency in their discipline. They motivate and guide students by being fair and rational. These classroom tactics require students to reflect on what they are seeing in the classroom in order to make decisions about how they should behave.

I find that SCT encourages people to consider the role of reflection in classrooms. While there are still many classroom management programs that focus on behavioral interventions (based on rewards and punishments), there are many others that focus on reflection. When students violate a rule, they might be asked to write a letter of apology or an essay in which they explain why the behavior was wrong or hurtful and how they could make another choice in the future.

Reflective activities can be used to manage bullying and other disrespectful behaviors. We want students to not just stop their behavior but also to learn why those bad behaviors are problematic and need to be changed. Behavior modification plans are not designed to stimulate the students' cognitive powers of reflection, while SCT can be seen as encouraging us to consider reflection as another process that affects learning.

So far, I have focused the discussion of SCT in the classroom on student behavior because that is an obvious and important application, but SCT is also important for understanding learning and motivation. Classrooms are inherently social and most teachers strive to use the social element to help students learn. Teachers model new procedures and skills to their students before having students model those procedures and skills for each other. Teachers try to orchestrate the classroom so that many sources of information encourage learning. From the resources available to the posters on the wall and the arrangement of desks, teachers are providing information to students about what is important to learn and what is helpful for learning.

In SCT, students' learning and motivational characteristics have been influenced by the classroom environment and by the behaviors in which the students have engaged. That is why it is important for teachers to continually assess whether these classroom-based elements are signaling the best behaviors to positively influence learning and motivation. Individuals will respond differently to the social environment, so teachers must simultaneously reflect on the whole class, while also monitoring individual students. Small adjustments typically need to be made throughout a school day so that learning can be maximized for all students. Such adjustments might help accommodate factors such as students' moods, needs for prerequisite knowledge before starting a new lesson, or needs for simplified or more explanatory instructions. Good teachers learn how to read the room and make the adjustments at the class level to reach most students.

SELF-DETERMINATION THEORY

The second big theory that I will summarize is Self-Determination Theory (SDT), which was developed by Ryan and Deci out of a body of research that dates back to the 1970s.[1,11] This theory holds that human agency is a requirement for success and well-being, and that having internalized reasons for behavior leads to success and happiness. There are five sub-theories within SDT, but for this book, I need only summarize three.

Three Tenets of SDT

One main tenet of SDT is that we need to recognize the distinction between intrinsic and extrinsic motivation, which I mentioned in Chapter 1. When we are intrinsically motivated, we follow a completely internalized reason for doing something. In fact, we experience enjoyment while engaged in an intrinsically motivated task or process. Extrinsically motivated tasks, on the other hand, are not completely internalized nor related to the task itself. For example, restaurant workers sometimes show up to work when they are ill because they are paid only when they show up. They do not enjoy working while sick and might not think it is even a good idea, but the external reward of the pay is enough to get them to work.

Given that there is extensive evidence in favor of intrinsically motivated behavior (e.g., more enjoyment, greater self-regulation, and higher achievement), we clearly want to encourage and promote intrinsic motivation in school and life in general.[1,2,3] However, we need experiences with different tasks before we are able to judge whether or not we enjoy them. We need to take courses, participate in lessons, and sample different hobbies before we can develop intrinsic motivation. We are likely going to have, and perhaps need, some extrinsic reasons for trying those courses, lessons, or hobbies. In other words, forcing or bribing ourselves—or others—to try something is not necessarily a bad tactic for initial motivation. I will say more about this when I introduce the internalization process of motivation. Let me be clear, though: I am not advocating extrinsic motivation for ongoing motivation. I am only stating that we might need to use extrinsic incentives, at times, to encourage students to try new or challenging learning activities.

In its second tenet, SDT highlights three basic needs that should be satisfied within a context before learners are most liable to experience intrinsic motivation in that context: autonomy, competence, and relatedness. We can see that there are clear implications for classrooms in this second tenet. The notion of autonomy reflects the need for personal agency or the feeling that one has some control within a situation. Competence is also related to agency since it is about whether we feel we can be effective and successful in a given situation. In the next chapter, I will discuss how competence and self-efficacy are similar constructs. The need for relatedness is about the importance of feeling personally connected within and to the situation. Often relatedness is about feeling that one belongs in that situation—that is, connected with the content of a situation, but more so with a sense of social belonging. Thus, SDT holds that positive motivation follows from need satisfaction.

The third key tenet of SDT is that there are gradations of external and internal motivation influenced by the three basic

Theoretical Underpinnings 23

needs described in the previous paragraph. Descriptions of these gradations can help us see how the process of internalization can lead to more positive motivation even when that motivation falls short of true intrinsic motivation. As noted previously, given what we know from everyday life, people need to be moved to action even when they are not intrinsically motivated. Otherwise, they might not be successful in school or work. I cannot show up for work only when I anticipate enjoying the day. We often need to persevere through challenge and boredom before we experience enjoyment. The earlier example of guitar lessons also fits here. Our student has to practice the same song repeatedly because she enjoys playing it when it finally sounds good. She can anticipate the intrinsic enjoyment and that keeps her motivated. There is a lot of work, much of which is not enjoyable, that goes into being able to play an instrument well.

According to SDT, we can use the internalization framework, shown in Figure 2.1, for thinking about how we regulate our behavior and/or the reasoning that underlies our choices of behaviors. As we look at the figure, we can see Amotivation to the left. In this case, we have neither reason nor intention to engage in the task, which clearly represents the absence of motivation. Someone may have started guitar lessons and then realized that s/he hated playing the instrument. This person likely will disengage in practice and not be concerned enough for any self-regulation. To the far right, we have Intrinsic Motivation, which represents the highest level of internalized motivation. Now the guitar player has reached a level of motivation that allows her to experience both enjoyment and satisfaction. In the middle of the figure, we have a continuum of Extrinsic Motivation that goes from completely external to more internalized. Importantly, we can

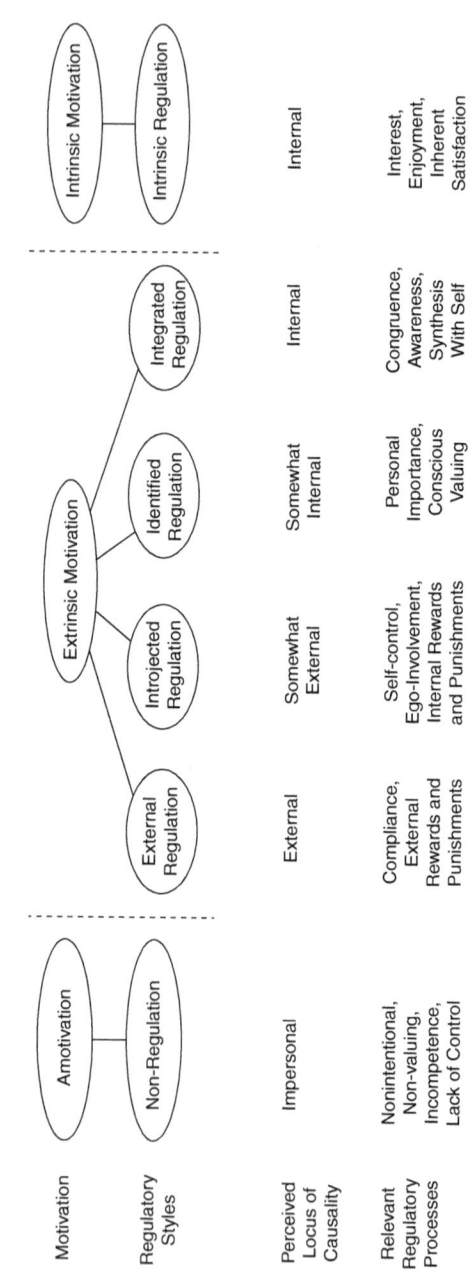

Figure 2.1 Self-Determination Continuum Showing Types of Motivation and Their Associated Regulatory Styles, Loci of Causality, and Regulatory Processes[1]

Theoretical Underpinnings 25

see that, as the motivation becomes more internalized, there is an increase in the valuing of the task and the self-regulation of behaviors related to completing the task. In fact, there is a significant difference between the guitar student who is bribed to practice by her mother and the one who has internalized the drive to be a better musician. Let's say that the mother of one student is paying the student a certain amount of money based on how many minutes she practices each week. The student working for this reward is not focusing her attention on how her proficiency might be improving. Instead, she is doing just enough to get the payment that she wants. Plus, if she discovers another way to make money, then she will lose her motivation to continue playing guitar. The student with introjected regulation is somewhat more internalized, but she is more focused on practicing so as to not feel guilty than on actual improvement. Avoiding guilt is not the same as having positive feelings about what you are doing. If she does not move beyond this level of internalizing, she might not have enough positive feeling toward playing guitar to keep it up. Once people start getting to the identified and integrated levels, they experience more internalized meaning related to the task itself (practicing guitar for improvement), which increases the value of the task and the potential for more genuinely positive feelings toward accomplishing the task. Future goals are reasons that can lead people to more internalized extrinsic regulation and help people experience success with tasks, like learning to play guitar, that require long periods of practice before expertise can be developed.

Another example of the internalization process is when people start a new exercise routine. Often people need to force or bribe themselves when it is time to get back on some exercise routine. Some people use tangible rewards to get started, like buying themselves something they want but do not need. After some time with the new routine, we internalize the impetus to do it. For some of us, it becomes important to our sense of self that we continue something that is healthy. We come to identify with having such a routine. For others, we start enjoying the routine and it no longer feels anything like a chore. However, there are still others who will keep exercising to avoid feeling guilty. Avoiding guilt is a more internalized reason than the completely external bribe, but it is not likely to yield positive affect toward the task or behavior. We do not normally enjoy the tasks we do simply out of guilt. The internalization of reasons for behaving certain ways or doing certain tasks is an important part of motivation and we shall see that it is integral to understanding the power of future goals.

Why SDT?

Before moving on, I want to point out that there are other theoretical frameworks, besides SDT, that I could use to establish the importance of future goals. Indeed, my initial research with future goals came from different theories.[12,13] For example, my colleagues and I were following the work on future time orientation[14,15] and future time perspective[16,17] when we first examined the role of future strivings. These are two related theories concerning how people's orientation toward the future could be found to influence their present motivation. While future time orientation is conceptualized as a unidimensional trait that captures the extent to which people are oriented toward their future, future time perspective examines multiple concepts related to how people view their futures and how those views influence their present strivings.[18] For example, in a review of that research, we found that women tended to see their future goals for education, career, and family as taking place in a relatively short amount of time and in close proximity to each other, while men tended to imagine their futures in terms of goals separated in time. The future goals themselves were similar, but the perspectives regarding their realization was different.[19]

The next iteration of our research with future goals was partially based on Expectancy-Value Theory,[20,21] which holds that students' performances, persistence, and choices can be predicted from knowing something about what they value about school tasks (the intrinsic enjoyment, the attainment, or the utility) and what they expect in regards to success or failure. We were interested in whether goals would be helpful in understanding performance if they were included in addition to the values.[20] The theory had two elements of future concern: utility value and expectancy. We found, with high school mathematics, that adding future goals did help with predicting both effort and achievement scores.

This brief history of my early future-oriented research is meant to show that there are other ways to theorize about future goals. I am not using either of those other perspectives because I discovered while teaching motivation to preservice teachers that using SDT made the practical applications much clearer. The continuum shown in Figure 2.1 helps illustrate how increases in internalization can result in more positive motivation and active regulation than when it is completely external (i.e., governed by rewards and punishments). Most people can readily recognize people, including themselves, who have behaved according to the different regulatory styles, depending on their external-versus-internal valuing of the activity. Teachers can also recognize that students can be encouraged with rewards, then nudged further along the continuum as they become engaged in trying to learn the content. The reason for encouraging future goals is easy to comprehend given SDT, and most teachers and parents will find such encouragement to be more realistic than encouraging intrinsic motivation. Intrinsic motivation is a journey that can be facilitated, but, given its internalized nature, the student must arrive there on his/her own. SDT makes these points more obvious to the lay person while the other theories may be more helpful to those doing research on these concepts.

Implications of SDT for the Classroom

It seems important to reflect on the implications of SDT generally for classrooms before moving on to the specific concepts of self-efficacy and future goals. At the simplest level, according to SDT, we want to set up our classrooms to prevent students from becoming or staying amotivated, and we want to encourage intrinsic motivation and guide our students toward experiencing some intrinsic motivation in our classes. More importantly, though, SDT gives us some good ideas about how to achieve these goals. First, we need to think about what we do in the classroom that can support student needs for autonomy, competence, and relatedness. An SDT researcher, Johnmarshall Reeve, has argued that autonomy-supporting teachers see their work as facilitating learning, rather than controlling students in the classroom.[22] Some teachers believe that they need to control students in order to instigate learning, but there is evidence that control more often undermines learning by undermining motivation to learn. In this section, I will summarize this perspective that Reeve developed based on reviewing research and inferring implications.

Autonomy-supporting teachers try to nurture the positive characteristics that students bring to the classroom and provide information that supports students' sense of autonomy and competence. They do this by providing choices whenever feasible (e.g., letting students choose topics and who to work with) and guiding them to complete moderately challenging tasks that build their sense of competence. When presenting lessons and the learning tasks within lessons, these teachers emphasize the values underlying the lesson/task and present rationales for learning the material. They also foster the need for relatedness by demonstrating their positive regard for all students and not allowing bullying or other hurtful behaviors in their classrooms. They cultivate the sense that everyone belongs to their classroom. These teachers acknowledge students' feelings, and even students' reluctance to engage with some tasks. This attunement to students' feelings signals to students that one is aware of their needs and cares about them.

According to Reeve, how teachers use language when presenting new tasks and giving feedback to students is very important for supporting positive motivation (which is more internalized motivation).[22] In my experience, students at all levels can infer when teachers are trying to control them. As I just noted, providing rationales to get students to consider why certain work needs to be done can help facilitate autonomy. You, as a teacher, are giving them information that helps them make effective choices about their schoolwork. You are also showing value for the task that the student might not have recognized on his/her own.

External rewards provided by teachers, however, can distract students from intrinsic motivation. I witnessed an example of this problem in a special education classroom. During a lively discussion of a current event topic, the teacher was giving classroom "bucks" whenever a student offered an opinion or comment, to encourage further participation. These classroom "bucks" could be exchanged for trinkets and privileges at a later time. While there is nothing wrong with using a system like that when students are not motivated, in the context of that discussion—in which many students wanted to participate—the use of the reward broke the flow of natural discussion. It was a moment of intrinsic learning and sharing that was undermined with external rewards.

One main hindrance to intrinsic academic motivation is that schools operate with many cues for extrinsic motivation (e.g., grades, stickers, behavior management systems), and it does not take long to make those more salient than intrinsic motivation. However, if a student was amotivated, then using the information from Figure 2.1, we might very well try a reward to get the student engaged minimally in schoolwork. Once we have a student engaging to some extent, meaning s/he is at least attempting to do the work in class, then we can figure out how to move that student further along the continuum toward more internalized motivation. Part of the job of a classroom teacher is to help students discover what interests them in the content and nurture their self-regulation so that they can enjoy their interests. Therefore, at the classroom level, we want to develop lessons around students' interests and goals, so that we generally are attempting to motivate all students toward internalized reasons for engaging in our lessons.

CONCLUSION

The point of Chapter 2 was to show that the concepts highlighted in this book are derived from two big theories that have been developed to help us understand why humans act the way they do and what helps people become more successful in governing their own lives. There are other related theories, but the book focuses on self-efficacy and future goals because of their links to self-regulation and successful performance. Thus, I chose to introduce SCT[6] and SDT[1,11] as two main theories that relate to these concepts. Theories can vary in terms of their relevance to practice, so I chose the two that I thought would be best for teachers and parents to understand how motivation can be encouraged.

I argued that SCT is a big theory that helps us understand how the self operates by using different sources of information that are interpreted, and then that interpretation encourages certain thoughts and actions that feed back into the self's understanding. The interpretive emphases and the reciprocal relationships are important for understanding human agency. Self-efficacy beliefs are developed based on the interpretive processes and then become part of the self-system that shapes behavior. Students in learning environments need information that helps them figure out how to behave successfully in that environment. Teachers need to be involved in helping students interpret the information in ways that promote continual learning and effective engagement with learning activities (i.e., the teacher's lessons). In the next chapter, we will see that persuasion is a key activity that teachers can use to help students maintain positive self-efficacy.

Although SCT is a clear theoretical home for the concept of self-efficacy, SCT does not as directly point to future goals. My contention is that one way to understand future goals is through the lens of SDT, a perspective likely to illuminate the how and why of future goals in a way that can be embraced by teachers and parents. Reflective and persistent engagement is imperative to internalizing reasons to engage in learning activities and to encouraging motivation in ourselves or others. We cannot make students more intrinsically motivated, but we can help students interpret the present situation as important or relevant to them. We can focus tasks on their interests and/or show them how the present task links to an important future goal. This can help students develop more internalized regulation. Future goals, in my opinion, are the next best thing to intrinsic motivation. Thus, they are the focus of Chapter 4. In the next chapter, though, I will attempt to thoroughly define and explain self-efficacy.

Three
Self-Efficacy

The purpose of this chapter is to clearly define self-efficacy and provide support for its importance for motivation to learn. We know, broadly, that there are many different facets related to motivation. Likewise, there are a number of different self-beliefs that are important for understanding the self-confidence aspect of motivation.[23,24,25] It is important to recognize how self-efficacy is different from other self-beliefs in order to understand why it was chosen for the focus of this book.

Research into motivation has found that perceptions can outweigh reality, to a certain extent. Earlier, I presented an example of a teacher who gave classroom "bucks" as incentives for student participation. Although the teachers may believe this to be motivating, some students are put off by what feels to them like manipulation. They perceive that their participation is being bought, or they experience the "money" as a distraction to their initial interest (and soon perceive the end goal as being accumulation of this fake money). In either case, the students' perception or experience of the practice undermines their motivation rather than supports it. Their perceptions do not match what the teacher intends. Motivation is, therefore, about what the student experiences and perceives rather than the intent of the teacher. This is why it is so important for teachers to observe how students respond to their attempts to encourage motivation and good behavior in the classroom. We have a similar situation with self-beliefs. A student may have shown you in his/her work that s/he can succeed in your math class, but still may have serious doubts about his/her ability in math. Perceptions of the self, especially in terms of competence, are integral to motivation to learn.[25]

HIERARCHY OF SELF-BELIEFS

We can think about the self-beliefs that concern competence in terms of levels of specificity or a hierarchy from general to specific.[23,24] Self-esteem is at the highest level of generality, and self-efficacy is the most specific level. Self-esteem captures a person's general sense of worth—regardless of context.[23,24] For example, I may think I am generally a good person, which means I have high self-esteem. Positive self-perceptions have been linked to happiness and lower anxiety. However, it has not been linked to academic achievement or pro-social behaviors despite efforts to find such links.[26,27] I will say more about that, after I define all three concepts.

Self-concept of ability lies in between self-esteem and self-efficacy in terms of a general-versus-specific assessment of self. Self-concept captures how we think and feel about ourselves in regards to domains or subjects.[23] Whereas self-esteem captures a very broad sense of self-worth, self-concept tends to focus on competence domains. Competence domains can be as broad as academics, athletics, and social relationships, or more specific content areas such as mathematics, science, music, and English/language arts.

Let me use myself as an example of self-concept of ability. I have never had a positive self-concept in sports or athletics, but within the domain of academics I generally had a high positive self-concept. More specifically, I had a high self-concept for subjects that involved a lot of reading and writing. When I engaged in these subjects I generally thought I was competent and felt good about my ability to perform or succeed. I had more neutral feelings in the domain of mathematics. My experiences in mathematics were of moderate success, but not much enjoyment. Self-concept is formed by considering how one's performance compares to others and how one feels about their performances (success and failures) in the domain. Clearly, it is more specific than one's general sense of self-esteem.

Self-efficacy, as noted in the first chapter, concerns one's confidence that s/he can learn something specific or complete a particular task. According to Bong and Clark,[23] self-efficacy is more focused on cognitive appraisals than self-concept, which includes both cognitive and affective information. In other words, self-efficacy is more about what I think of my ability to be successful with some task, while self-concept of ability includes both thoughts and feelings about myself performing in some domain or content area. So, a student, when exhibiting or assessing self-efficacy, is focused on whether s/he can accomplish a particular task or achieve a certain outcome. Within the specific context, however, there is still room for levels of specificity. For instance, I may have high self-efficacy for passing a particular class, getting an A in that class, or for completing a portion of an exam within that class.

Therefore, self-efficacy is a more specific perception than the belief that one is good or bad at math. Think of our example of the seventh-grade student, Jenice, who has always done well in math but is new to algebra. She might have a high self-concept of ability for math, which means she is generally confident about her math ability and positive about learning math, but she can still lack confidence as she anticipates her first algebra exam. Research suggests that we would want to help Jenice use her positive self-concept in math to build positive self-efficacy for her algebra exam. Having high self-concept in a domain and high self-efficacy for tasks predicts achievement. We cannot assume that a math-confident student will have high self-efficacy when confronted with a subject like algebra that appears new to her.

A study by Mimi Bong and colleagues, published in 2012, demonstrated these relationships with elementary and middle school Korean students studying mathematics (study 1) and mathematics and language arts (study 2).[24] They examined links from measures of four levels of self-constructs (two for self-efficacy) to measures of anxiety, task value (motivation for the task), and achievement. They wanted to see if there were direct links to achievement and indirect links via anxiety and motivation. They found, in study 1, that all four measures of self were related to task value and anxiety. Three of the four also had direct links to achievement. Global self-esteem was not linked to achievement in mathematics. These findings were replicated in their study 2, though there was a small association from global self-esteem to achievement in language arts. Ultimately, the measures of self that asked about a domain (math or language arts) had more predictive power in explaining the achievement of students in those subjects. It is not that feeling good about oneself generally is what matters for learning, but rather being confident and positive relative to a domain that one is studying. Importantly, these findings replicated very similar findings with western samples from the United States.

Before I leave behind the topic of global self-esteem, I will present several examples that I think explain why being precise in language use when moving from educational research

Self-Efficacy 37

to practice is important. Starting in the 1970s, educators and politicians sought to improve educational outcomes by promoting self-esteem.[26,27] This was during a period when low self-esteem was being blamed for academic failure, bullying, drug use, and other outcomes that society considers to be negative. It was not a huge stretch to think that bolstering self-esteem might be a positive avenue for reaching out to struggling youth, especially in urban areas. However, there was no solid evidence that self-esteem was causally related to any outcomes. California was one state that embraced self-esteem programming in their K–12 schools. They were able to demonstrate positive effects on self-esteem, but there were no other positive effects of the program. Instead, the findings suggested that the program helped separate self-esteem from success in school. Meaning that it was easier to feel good about one's self, even in the face of failure at school, following completion of the self-esteem program. One can argue about whether or not this is a problematic finding. I fall on the side of it being problematic because school failure has long-term negative consequences for most people, so we want students to at least care about their schooling.

A more recent study looked at this phenomenon with college students.[28] Forsyth and colleagues conducted an experiment in a large college class in which students earning Cs, Ds, and Fs were given either self-esteem-bolstering feedback, study strategy ideas, or no feedback (i.e., the control). They found that the D and F students actually performed more poorly following the self-esteem feedback. Separating one's global sense of self from his/her academic performance, we conclude, does not help improve academic performance.

Since the 1980s, when the California experiment in self-esteem promotion was conducted, a significant amount of work has shown that global self-esteem does not predict academic achievement (or lowered drug use, less bullying, etc.). I have relied on the work of Roy Baumeister (and his colleagues) to understand these findings.[26,27] That work encourages people to move away from a focus on self-esteem. At the same time, there has been ample evidence demonstrating the importance of both self-concept and self-efficacy.[29]

FOCUSING ON SELF-EFFICACY

The choice to focus this book on self-efficacy over self-concept of ability was largely motivated by the significant amount of evidence that self-efficacy matters for academic motivation and success. Self-efficacy is also a relatively straightforward concept which better enables teachers and parents to readily grasp its meaning. I say this because there are other concepts related to motivation that I still struggle to comprehend after studying motivation for more than 20 years! There are clear implications for teachers and classrooms, however, in regard to self-efficacy.

Self-efficacy is based on how people judge whether or not they are able to engage in the activities needed to achieve a particular goal, in a particular context. Therefore, self-efficacy beliefs are context-specific and future-oriented judgments (Can I do it?). Self-efficacy beliefs also vary in terms of level or degree (How confident am I, given the degree of difficulty in the task?).[29] It is important to note that—given the specific nature of self-efficacy beliefs—we must consider generality, or the extent to which self-efficacy beliefs can generalize to similar tasks. Research has shown that, although the closer the self-efficacy belief is to the actual target task, the better the prediction, there is still meaningful prediction when the belief is more general than the target task.[23,24,29,30] For example, if you give a student a math worksheet, his/her efficacy judgment for that worksheet will be a good predictor of his/her ability to complete the worksheet. If I ask him/her how confident s/he generally is in completing the math activities in the fourth grade, that assessment will predict (to some extent) how the student performs on different assessments in that math class. If that were not the case, we would, arguably, be less interested in the concept of self-efficacy.[30]

To provide further clarity on the concept of self-efficacy, let me show you some sample items used in research. A common item would be, "I am sure I have the ability to understand the ideas and skills taught in this course." Another sample item is, "I am certain I can understand the material presented in this class." Note that there is a reference to the context in the item. In much of our work, we have used classes as the level of generality.[10] We asked students to frame their responses to our questions relative to either "the current class" or "their current math classes." Our goal is to get students thinking about the context in which we want to understand their motivation. Therefore, we preface the self-efficacy items with instructions to think about their performance in the class or context in which we are interested. Otherwise, we tend to lose predictive power. For example, when trying to determine Jenice's self-efficacy for the new algebra class, we must stimulate her thinking about that class and not just about math classes in general. We know that her self-concept of ability in math is fairly strong, but that will not help us understand whether she will struggle with efficacy issues in the new algebra class.

To summarize the definition of self-efficacy: Self-efficacy is a person's degree of confidence that s/he can successfully do something or learn something. As an example, the guitar student looks at a new piece of music and judges the likelihood that she can learn it during the next month. She assesses the difficulty and judges the degree of her confidence. To the extent that her self-efficacy is high, she will more likely attempt to learn the new piece. Evidence has shown that self-efficacy in learning situations is central to helping us understand what people will choose to try, how much effort they will put forth, and the degree to which they will perceive having control over the learning.[29,31]

WHERE DOES SELF-EFFICACY COME FROM?

The next issue we should consider is how students develop their self-efficacy, and how teachers and parents can help. To understand the issue of development, let's go back to the work of Bandura,[4,5,29] who first proposed that self-efficacy is shaped by the student's perception of cues in the social context in which the task is being learned or performed. The most powerful cue is past experience with the same or similar tasks. In particular, past mastery experiences are the strongest influence on high self-efficacy for any task. An old adage, success breeds success, applies here. However, there is an important caveat: The student must recognize that success occurred and that s/he was the agent of that success. This leads to another source of self-efficacy: persuasion by others. This is not as powerful as past experience, but it may help students interpret their past experiences in ways that support their ongoing motivation. Teachers, coaches, and parents need to help some students see that they succeeded due to their own efforts and abilities. People's interpretations of their own experiences may be different from what a teacher, coach, or parent perceives. A student who struggles with low self-efficacy may need help attributing successes to his/her own actions. Ultimately, those internal attributions for success should feed back into supporting more positive self-efficacy.[31,32]

So far, we have noted that past experiences and persuasion by others are important for developing self-efficacy. Although these are probably the most relevant, we should understand the other two as well: vicarious experience and physiological responses.[4,29,31] The concepts of modeling behaviors and social learning are central to the notion of people obtaining self-efficacy information from vicarious experience. We watch how people do in different situations and size up whether our experience will be similar or different. If someone very different from us fails at a task that we are thinking about doing, we are not likely to experience diminished motivation. If that same person knocked it out of the ballpark, we also will not likely experience enhanced self-efficacy. However, if someone similar to us has great success, we are likely to be encouraged and perhaps develop sufficient self-efficacy to attempt that new task. We can revisit the example of our guitar student to understand how vicarious experience works. As I mentioned in Chapter 1, neither Andrés Segovia nor Jimi Hendrix would be sufficient models to motivate the novice guitar player because their expertise is too advanced for her to realistically derive self-efficacy information. Additionally, they are both men and the similarity of the model is important, though not only in regards to gender. The guitar teacher searching for a role model would be well-advised to find a female guitar player of an age similar to our example student who is more accomplished than our student, and who continues to develop her expertise. That player is likely to be a powerful model when the teacher uses vicarious experience to encourage the student. While the student may love to listen to both Segovia and Hendrix, they may not be the best models for when she experiences a high or new challenge and needs a self-efficacy boost to help her persist.

I would also like to remind the reader of the example algebra student, Jenice. Recall that, in this example, we have a student who has done well in math thus far and has a positive self-concept of ability in math, but she is taking her first algebra exam. Jenice will look more closely to her success and challenges in the work in this class than rely on her self-concept of ability. The teacher or parent may need to use persuasion to help her bridge positive self-concept to positive self-efficacy for the exam. This is especially useful if she has been uncertain about her performance on the work she has done in algebra class prior to the exam. She would benefit from being able to see another girl in the class be successful, according to self-efficacy theory.

One of the most important aspects of motivation is that it helps us work through challenges, or persist when we experience some event or task as a daunting challenge. Whether it is an outright failure or a perceived setback, we need to find the motivation to get over it and to move on. When we see other people rise up to face their setbacks, we can derive some support for our own self-efficacy. That is one way in which vicarious experiences can inform the development of self-efficacy. "Comeback" stories are so appealing because we garner inspiration from them—they provide vicarious information that redemption or recovery following failure is possible.

In addition to past mastery experiences, social persuasion, and vicarious experiences, we interpret our physiological responses, or emotional arousal, in situations to gain information about our self-efficacy.[4] Those interpretations can help or hinder our self-efficacy. Sometimes when we feel our heart rate increasing and our palms beginning to sweat, we can tell ourselves that we are "pumped" and ready for the upcoming task. Often, though, strong physiological signals create anxiety that lowers our self-efficacy. This is why teachers will often try to convince students to relax prior to an important test. The guitar student may use relaxation to either help her feel efficacious about performing or teach herself to positively frame the heightened emotional arousal as indicating her readiness and excitement for the performance. It is easy to see why athletic coaches focus on the positive aspect of physiological excitement, as they want the energy to be available for the performance, geared toward positive self-efficacy rather than anxiety and doubt.

CLASSROOM IMPLICATIONS: WHAT ARE GOOD PRACTICES TO SUPPORT SELF-EFFICACY?

Now that we have examined the concept from the perspective of our two individual learners, let us examine the implications at the classroom level. There are some general recommendations to present before we can explore the issues within classroom scenarios (I will leave the details of that discussion for Chapter 5, so that I can tie the two concepts together in their applications to classrooms). The general recommendations described below were previously summarized by Urdan and Turner in a chapter from the *Handbook on Competence and Motivation* based on their review of research on how different concepts related to student competence manifest in classrooms.[33] My comments focus more specifically on self-efficacy, and I have summarized them in Table 3.1.

As noted previously, classrooms are inherently social environments; therefore, we need to understand how the teacher can orchestrate that environment to provide students with support for positive self-efficacy. First, instruction needs to be well-designed to match the incoming needs of the students. The best, most powerful support for self-efficacy is actual mastery (successful learning) experiences. Students need to have successful learning experiences and be told that they are responsible for those successes.

Second, to be successful and motivated, students need to tackle tasks of moderate difficulty. When learning tasks are too easy, there is no feeling of accomplishment to bolster self-efficacy. In fact, easy tasks might signal to students that the teacher does not think they can handle more difficult work. If the tasks are too challenging, that makes it easy for students to give up. Moderate challenge shows students that they are learning new knowledge and skills, and gives them a sense of accomplishment that can bolster their self-efficacy.

Third, teachers should develop and use assessments of their students' knowledge and self-efficacy in order to help meet the students' needs. Much of the graded work teachers use during instruction (seatwork, homework, projects, quizzes, exams) can be tweaked to gain efficacy information. For example, they can add two questions about how confident students were while completing the assignment. Teachers typically use their graded work to assess students' knowledge, but they should also use those assessments to change the instruction if the work seems too easy or too difficult.

I need to pause my listing of recommendations to point out that what I have been describing thus far is consistent with the idea that effective teaching involves differentiated instruction. By differentiated instruction, I mean the practice of planning lessons around the idea that students within a given class are going to have different strengths and weaknesses to make learning more accessible. When learning is more accessible, more students experience mastery of the content. Much motivation research, in my opinion, points to the need for differentiated instruction. Although it may seem that school administrators have only recently started talking about it, differentiated instruction is a topic that Carol Ann Tomlinson has been writing about since the mid-1990s. Her work is grounded in research but written for teachers.[34]

Returning to the list of recommendations, it is important to note that students' sense of competence develops with a sense of control over their learning. The fourth recommendation, then, is to encourage student autonomy in the classroom. Allow them to make choices, set goals, and make decisions about how to get their schoolwork done. Although younger students need more guidance, students at all levels benefit from practice with goal-setting and decision-making. Classrooms that are tightly controlled by the teacher generally do not allow students ample opportunities to develop skills that encourage self-regulation. Feeling control over learning and becoming more self-regulated, in turn, supports student self-efficacy.

A fifth recommendation, related to the fourth one, is to provide students with feedback on their work that is highly informational rather than controlling or only evaluative (as in good, poor, etc.). Students need to know the strengths of their work, along with what needs correction. We want to focus their attention on where they are showing improvement in their knowledge and skills related to the graded assignment, as well as where they still need to improve relative to that knowledge and those skills. Controlling teacher messages focus on compliance to rules and indicate the teacher's need for compliance rather than attention to student learning. Oftentimes, teachers inadvertently signal compliance by awarding points for following guidelines and for clearly trying to please the teacher.

Personally, I still find this issue of giving informational feedback challenging, even after decades of teaching. When

I have many papers to grade (which is often), I struggle to provide meaningful feedback to each student. As a general plan, I designate some assignments during a grading period for informational feedback that is personalized for each student. On the other assignments, I give more summary feedback on how I see the group improving and include examples of good improvement. I explain this to students and tell them that I will gladly meet with them for individual conferences to discuss any of their work.

A sixth recommendation is to help students focus on their own work, their own progress, and the processes through which they are learning and meeting their goals. We want to discourage students from making comparisons with their peers. Students naturally size up themselves relative to others. According to social learning theory, this is a natural enough part of being human that teachers do not need to further encourage peer competition to support student efficacy. Competition can add fun to a classroom when used in that spirit, but competition for grades and public accolades has a demotivating effect for many students. For example, when a teacher only displays "best work" in the classroom, and the same students always have their work displayed, that sends a blatant message that some students will never have their work displayed. It also tells the top performers that they can relax because everyone knows they are at the top. Every student has room to grow in any content area, and we do not want to send messages about anyone being "done learning" just because they outperform other students in the current class. Of course, there are some students who will not be discouraged in the face of peer comparisons, but given that many will be (at both the bottom and top of performance) and given that people naturally compare themselves to others,

Table 3.1 Six Recommendations for Supporting Self-Efficacy in the Classroom

	Recommendation	Explanation
1	Set students up for mastery experiences.	Tailor instruction to meet the students' needs so that they can have success learning the material.
2	Provide students with learning tasks at moderate levels of challenge.	Make sure the tasks are not too hard or too easy. Monitor for frustration and signs of boredom.
3	Develop and use assessments of learning and motivation to plan and revise lessons.	Assessments should be ongoing; use daily assignments, projects, quizzes, and exams to garner information about where students are currently in their understanding. Items asking about self-efficacy should be added to typical assessments.
4	Encourage autonomy and control.	Provide students with choices about topics and assignments. Guide them toward making good decisions about their learning.
5	Provide feedback that is more informational than controlling.	Feedback on work submitted should indicate where students are improving and what skills need more improvement. Should not emphasize whether the teacher is pleased with the student's performance.

there is no need for teachers to make this a part of their classroom structure. There are other ways to display examples of good work. For example, teachers can have students select their own best work to display. The overall point is that, in general, all students need to keep their focus on what they are accomplishing and how they can reach their goals.

CONCLUSION

In this chapter I argued that self-efficacy should not be confused with self-esteem or self-concept of ability, but especially not self-esteem because it does not help us understand who will be successful or not successful in academic settings. For this book, motivation to learn is the focus and self-efficacy has been found over and over again to help us understand positive motivation to learn and successful learning.[4,6,23,24,25] Self-efficacy refers to the degree to which someone is confident that s/he is capable of learning or being successful in some context.

There are four sources of information that people use to evaluate their self-efficacy. The most powerful source is past experiences with the same or similar tasks. In particular, if a student has the experience of mastery in the past, his/her self-efficacy is likely to be high, assuming s/he owns that past mastery experience. Sometimes students do not see their own agency in their experiences. That is where the second source of information comes into play. Social persuasion can be used to bolster self-efficacy, and often the person attempting persuasion will try to show a student that s/he was successful in the past due to his/her own efforts and ability. We also use vicarious experience to inform our self-efficacy. We observe other people's successes and failures (and the consequences) and assess the similarity of those experiences to our own.

As teachers and parents, we need to take care in choosing models for our students. For role models to work, they have to seem both familiar and positive before the vicarious experience can be helpful. Finally, I noted that we also interpret our physiological responses to experiences and take these interpretations into consideration when forming our self-efficacy. Note that the process of interpretation is very important. We construct our self-efficacy based on our perceptions of what we and others have experienced. Teachers and parents can help students interpret those experiences in positive ways that encourage high self-efficacy.

Four
Future Goals

The concept of self-efficacy was introduced first because of the depth of evidence that it is an essential ingredient to positive motivation. People need to believe that they are capable of successfully tackling new skills, new tasks, and new learning. Beyond self-efficacy, however, people also need a good reason for trying something new or persevering with something difficult. We can call these reasons goals. In this chapter I will define and provide evidence for the importance of *future goals*. Future goals (also called future consequences in the research literature) refer to situations when the reason for doing a current task is motivated by the belief that the task is instrumental to obtaining something important in the future.[12,13,18]

DEFINING FUTURE GOALS

Future goals, in the current conceptualization, are a type of task-specific goal. Task-specific goals capture the reasons people report for doing the work required in a particular setting.[24,25] For the purposes of this book, the settings will relate to learning, as they were in the discussion of self-efficacy. When we talk about task-specific goals, the specificity issue is similar to what it was for the discussion of self-efficacy—that is, there needs to be some congruity between the context and the goal. For example, if I am an elementary teacher who wants to encourage her students to work on a mathematics assignment, I will explain to them why this math information will be useful *later on*, so that the future utility or need becomes a reason to complete the work. That is distinct from telling students that good grades are dependent on their completion of the work (which is a broader reason for doing the work). It is also distinct from merely telling them that math is a generally important school subject. In place of those broader reasons, the current work or task can be connected to the future utility for that knowledge or those skills. Those broader issues are also important and may motivate some students, but future goals are a way to make a concrete connection between current efforts and a future payoff. The payoff might be academic (success on the next math topic), or personal (helping a student figure out how to make his/her allowance go further).

In addition to motivating the current work in school settings, there is another motivation angle to future goals that should not be overlooked. When teachers talk to students about how current behaviors link to future goals, they are encouraging self-regulation.[9,12] Future goals help students see the connection between the present and future and may get students thinking about whether or not their current level of engagement will yield that future payoff. In our work with high school students learning mathematics, we found that students who reported having future goals for their classes also reported more regulated engagement in those classes.[12,20]

A lot of the research on motivation to learn has focused on achievement goals or goals, such as learning/mastery and performance goals, which capture people's concern about their competence in achievement situations.[35,36,37,38,39] Sometimes people focus on whether they are learning enough or gaining sufficient competence in the learning situation. These goals are learning or mastery goals. People with these goals report that they are trying to learn as much as they can, so their focus is on how to gain competence and learn new skills. An example item from research that measures these goals is, "I do the work in this class because I want to improve my understanding of the ideas and/or skills."[39] With performance goals, the reasons for doing the work in an achievement context are more about appearing competent to others and competing well. An example item is, "I do the work in this class because I like to perform better than other students."[39] Performance goals are more about the appearance of competence rather than actual mastery of any content. Achievement goals are further parsed into whether the goal is to approach something desired or to avoid something unwanted.[36,37,38] Wanting to perform or achieve more than others is an approach goal, while wanting to avoid a negative evaluation from a performance is an avoidance goal. Performance avoidance goals are particularly problematic for motivation because they are undergirded by a high fear of failure and low confidence of success. An example of a performance avoidance goal item is, "The reason I work in my class is so that others in the class won't think I'm dumb."[38]

Although the available evidence concludes that achievement goals are important for learning, achievement goals are also more complicated both theoretically and practically. For example, there is an ongoing debate about whether or not performance approach goals are helpful or detrimental to motivation in the classroom.[10,37] There is also a long history of concerns about how performance goals have been measured.[10] I have decided to avoid the complexity and controversy and instead focus on another type of task-specific goal, future goals, which are more straightforward to describe and too often overlooked.[12,13,40] Research on motivation to learn focuses less frequently on future goals, despite that they have been deemed important for learning and can be easily understood by teachers, parents, and students. Thus, I have chosen to write about future goals rather than achievement goals.

Before moving on from this point about achievement goals, I should clarify why I chose future goals over mastery goals for this book given the evidence that mastery goals lead to successful learning. The short answer is that mastery goals have been extensively covered, and one cannot talk about them without also including performance goals, which have mixed and complicated findings. However, there is also a more practical reason why I have chosen to focus on future goals rather than mastery goals. I believe that, by focusing on future goals, we might be able to encourage more students to internalize their reasons for studying and their attempts to learn. For one thing, it should be easier to get students to embrace future goals than to get them to adopt mastery goals. Like intrinsic motivation, mastery goals are the gold standard of goals given the level of engagement they stimulate in students. Teachers should encourage them, but many students will not reach that level of motivation given that there are so many signals in life that distract students from seeking mastery learning. However, if we help learners understand how their current schoolwork is related to something they value in the long term, they could move further along the self-determination framework shown in Figure 2.1, which means they will value the learning more and work harder. This will allow them to more fully grasp the content that will help them in the future. I believe that as teachers and parents we could be doing more to bridge the gap between fully externalized regulation and fully internalized regulation, and the evidence supports instructors encouraging future goals as a means of bridging that gap.

Let us consider a classroom scenario that might better explain the differences between mastery and future goals. I know a fifth-grade teacher who loves to create science lessons with an eye toward encouraging intrinsic motivation (which will also encourage mastery goals). He uses students' interests in his lessons to show them that the work will be challenging but doable (which also supports their self-efficacy), allows ample time for them to work with the lesson materials, and models his own enthusiasm while teaching. For some students, this will get them excited to learn and genuinely engage in the lessons. However, although this teacher is correctly applying positive motivation strategies, not all of his students will adopt learning/mastery goals. For some students, the science lessons are complex enough that they will doubt their ability to earn the best grades that they expect and want. They are the students who are always asking about how grades will be determined and how they can earn the A they want. They are distracted by their desire/need for a high grade and want to do what they need for that extrinsic goal. Other students, meanwhile, are simply not interested in either the content or the grade in science and will try to do even less than the students who are distracted by grades. These same students might be very positively motivated in math and/or language arts, but they are just not interested in science. This describes a very normal fifth-grade classroom in terms of motivation. If we were to persuade the students who do not have mastery goals that the current science lessons will help them with some future goal (such as the next math lesson, doing well overall in the fifth grade, middle school science, etc.), then they might buy into the importance of learning and try harder than they would otherwise. Lessons need to be pitched to students in multiple ways so that the teacher increases the likelihood that more students will find the lesson relevant. Relevance encourages students to internalize, thereby increasing their efforts to learn.

I would also like to return to the point about people needing reasons for attempting to learn in addition to having sufficiently high self-efficacy. I believe the best way to grasp this point is to return to both the guitar and math examples. Let's say that a teenaged guitar student has progressed particularly well in classical style and her teacher is encouraging her to participate in a recital. Although she knows she is capable of performing at a recital, she is afraid that her friends and family will make fun of her. Most of her family and friends are country music fans who would likely find classical music pretentious. This is what we call a negative outcome expectation. An outcome expectation is different from either a goal or a self-efficacy assessment. These expectations capture what we expect to experience after we do something. In this case, after the recital, the student expects unpleasant teasing and feelings of embarrassment rather than congratulations and feelings of pride. However, if she had a goal that was very important to her, that might be a stronger motivation than avoiding the expected negative outcome. Importantly, though, her hesitation is not due to low self-efficacy. The point is that we need to explore multiple reasons for why students hesitate when we think they should embrace opportunities to shine and show the results of their successful learning.

In academic settings, such as math, we can have a similar situation in which low self-efficacy is not the motivation problem, but rather the student's anticipation of a negative outcome following their attempts to do well. Some students have high self-efficacy but shy away from attempting to excel because they might be teased or shunned by others. When students have friends who think that school is not "cool," the stigma of being a math geek or a nerd can discourage them from trying. However, if students also have meaningful goals, those goals will compete with the negative outcome expectation and perhaps win. Thus, students need goals related to the learning context that will mitigate against, or challenge, any negative outcome expectations. Of course, we can also try to directly dispel negative outcome expectations, but in either case, holding a goal that competes against the negative will be useful, and a future goal can offer a powerful challenge.

CONCEPT OF INSTRUMENTALITY

In this section, I am going to explain the role that instrumentality plays in making future goals relevant. It is important to recognize that goals and values that are extrinsic to a given task are not uniformly motivating. Nor do they uniformly hinder motivation. From SDT and the research that supports it, we can further understand the different roles that extrinsic incentives can play in motivation.[1] Reviewing the figure presented in Chapter 2, we see that the internalization of self-regulation processes is related to the degree to which incentives or motives are externalized (or internalized). When the task is being done for a completely external incentive, such as when a student studies math because her parents give money for As on math tests, the effort is the least self-regulated. That means that the student will put forth the effort needed to get the money, but she is not reflecting on whether or not she is learning. Her attention is on the money rather than on the material. This may be sufficient for short-term success in math, but it does not sustain effort or learning over time. If she were to get a job that pays a similar amount, she has no reason to continue studying. If we can get her to internalize the importance of the task itself—that is, learning math in this example—then she is more likely to sustain her efforts to learn. According to SDT (see Figure 2.1), we want people to experience, at least, identified regulation so that there will be personal relevance in completing tasks that are not intrinsically rewarding.[1]

Research has demonstrated that when people recognize the instrumentality of a task to achieving a goal that is meaningful, they are more likely to persist with the task and put forth necessary effort, which then leads to more successful learning.[12,13,18,40] Miller and Brickman developed a model that demonstrates how this works.[41] The idea is that when people realize that their current efforts are related to that meaningful goal, they are more likely to try to develop subgoals that will leverage the present context to achieve that other, more distant goal. A distant future goal, in and of itself, can be insufficient for maintaining motivation. In fact, if we only hold the distant goal in mind, we are unlikely to achieve it unless we also set proximal goals that lead to it. Weight loss is a great example of this. If we only focus on the overall goal of losing, say, 50 pounds, we are unlikely to reach that goal. Instead, we need to break the 50-pound total down to weekly goals that are more concrete and realistic—perhaps a pound a week. Miller and Brickman argued that future goals encourage people to develop their proximal goals and the strategies to achieve them. Unless we have the future goal to lose weight, we will not start the plan to lose a pound a week.

I should note here that when I refer to future goals in this book, I am assuming future goals that stimulate perceived instrumentality. Without the link from the current learning to the future goal, the goals are likely to be too abstract to influence classroom motivation. The research literature on future goals uses multiple terms that are largely interchangeable. For example, in our early work we used the term future consequences.[12] An example survey item from that research was, "I do the work in this class because good grades lead to other things that I want (e.g., money, graduation, college acceptance or scholarships, eligibility for extracurricular activities)." In our subsequent work, we used the same items but we referred to either future goals[20] or perceived instrumentality.[12,39] Example items in that research are, "I do the work in this class because my performance in this class is important for becoming the person I want to be" and "I do the work in this class because mastering the ideas and skills taught in this class will help me in the future." You can see that despite the differences in terminology reflected in the different survey items, the current schoolwork is being linked to valued future goals. In research articles, we now prefer the term perceived instrumentality because it most closely communicates what the measurement scales used in research are precisely measuring. When students are able to see that the current schoolwork is important to reaching a valued or personally meaningful future goal, they are more motivated and engaged in that work. I chose to describe this general idea with the term "future goals" for this book because it is more straightforward for an audience of preservice and practicing teachers.

There are other concepts in the research on motivation that are similar to future goals, such as extrinsic utility values and extrinsic valuing. In Chapter 2 I referred to Expectancy-Value Theory,[21] which examines values that are intrinsic and extrinsic. Examples of extrinsic utility value items are, "How useful is learning advanced high school math for what you want to do after you graduate and go to work? (not very useful, very useful)" and "How useful is what you learn in advanced high school math for your daily life outside school? (not at all useful, very useful)." In our work in which we included values, we also used the following item for extrinsic valuing: "Learning this material is important because of its future value." These valuing items are different in subtle ways from future goal items and can add to our understanding of achievement.

It turns out that much of the research on future goals has sought to illustrate that they are an independent source of motivation.[40] In our research we have found that the future goal items explain variation in achievement and effort in addition to other variables including achievement goals and values.[12,13,20,39] In other words, future goals add to our understanding of what motivates people in ways that are unique to other goals and self-efficacy. More specifically, in two different studies of high school math classes we found that future goals and self-efficacy predicted effort and achievement.[12,20] In a college class we found that future goals predicted self-regulation, effort, and achievement after the role of other goals was accounted for in a prediction equation.[13] My colleagues and I, along with other researchers, found that future goals were related to–but distinct from–task values (i.e., reports that the effort is worthwhile, or the learning is useful).[13,20,42] In a study with high school language arts students, we found that future goals and self-efficacy both predicted mastery goals and strategy use (effort) and that those directly predicted course performance.[39] Finally, Vansteenkiste, Lens, and Deci reviewed a series of studies and concluded that the crux of why future goals were motivating was that they linked the current endeavor to personally meaningful future goals.[43] They presented strong evidence that linking the present to intrinsic future goals, such as personal growth, well-being, and having healthy relationships (rather than wealth and fame) was most influential for affecting positive engagement. When people can see the relevance to personally meaningful outcomes, they are more likely to be internally regulated and significantly engaged in the task at hand. The finding of intrinsic future goals being more positive than extrinsic future goals was also supported in a study by Tabachnick, Miller, and Relyea.[44]

CLASSROOM IMPLICATIONS: WHAT ARE GOOD PRACTICES TO ENCOURAGE FUTURE GOALS?

Although there is not much research on how teachers can use future goals in the classroom, there are some common-sense ideas that can be easily inferred from what we do know about these goals. I will be discussing this at length in Chapter 5, but I also want to present some implications here. In Table 4.1, I summarize five recommendations that are supported by the theory and research on classroom motivation.

CONCLUSION

One conclusion of this chapter is that while self-efficacy is a concept that must be distinguished from concepts that seem similar (self-esteem), future goals should be equated with the concept of perceived instrumentality. Future goals refer to when there is a personally valued future goal that is seen as connected to the current situation. Perceived instrumentality is when the present task is linked to something important that one is striving to achieve. The recognition of that relationship inspires people to figure out strategies that will create a path from the present to that future goal.[41] Research has shown that having these future goals enhances the quality

Table 4.1 Five Recommendations for Supporting Future Goals in the Classroom

	Recommendation	Explanation
1	Learn about your students and their future goals.	Find out how they view the future and what is meaningful to them. For some, the future might be the next test, or the next class. For others, it might be staying eligible for sports. Still others might be planning for their careers.
2	Introduce lessons in multiple ways.	Make a pitch for lessons in multiple ways such as interesting, fun, useful, new, etc. Not all students will see your reason, but they are likely to see a reason for trying to learn, if you give them multiple options or reasons to consider.
3	Focus their attention on the more internalized reasons for doing the work in your class.	Help them focus on the relevance of learning the material. Students tend to already have extrinsic and performance goals, so we do not need to encourage those. Instead, we should encourage them to see the personal relevance so that they will work harder to learn the material.
4	Encourage self-regulation.	Teach students goal setting and monitoring progress toward goals. Allow them to make choices and experience the consequences of their choices.
5	Model your own efforts to achieve goals.	Students need to see how adults manage their continued learning and working toward goals. Teachers should talk to students about how they work toward their meaningful future goals.

of engagement and degree of self-regulation that people will show in the current context. The work of Vansteenkiste et al. and Tabachnick et al. further suggests that future goals that are linked to personal relevance were stronger motivators than those that linked to money and/or status.[43,44] The implications for motivation to learn in classrooms will be discussed further in Chapter 5.

Five
Implications for Motivating Others

In this fifth chapter, I will explore more fully the implications of the two concepts for understanding motivation. We should care about these two concepts because they help us think about why students might not be motivated and they provide us with concrete ideas on how to help students find more productive motivation. I will explore these implications first with our examples of individuals, then with classroom examples.

When people talk about students being motivated or unmotivated, they are generally making inferences based on what they observe in terms of engagement (willingness or reluctance to engage), affect (positive or negative), time spent (as in persistence or lack thereof), and effort (perfunctory versus meaningful). In fact, we can gather a lot of evidence about motivation to learn by watching how people approach new learning tasks. There are two points that we need to keep in mind while observing people: 1) People are motivated—they seek to satisfy their basic needs; and 2) The meaning of one's current motivation resides within the individual. Our inferences about others can easily be wrong unless we explore, with the individual, how s/he is motivated. We must talk to students to understand what is really going on with their motivation. When students are clearly not motivated to undertake a learning activity, something else may be more motivating to them, and it might be instructive to identify their preoccupation.

Motivation comes from perceptions of experiences, and we often need to help people (students, children, friends) frame their experiences in ways that encourage positive, ongoing motivation. What does this mean for self-efficacy and future goals? I chose to focus on self-efficacy and future goals because I think of these two facets of motivation as relatively straightforward and malleable. We can understand how they influence people. Low self-efficacy makes us reluctant to try and hesitant to persist, while salient future goals encourage us to try and to persist. Let's revisit our two examples of individuals, starting with the guitar player.

EXAMPLES WITH INDIVIDUALS

As the story unfolds, we find that the guitar player has continued with both classical and rock music, with rock guitar being the newer genre for her. Her teacher tells her that she has to play with other musicians or her talent cannot further develop. Since she has played solo classical for a long time, she has low self-efficacy for playing rock music in a group. Indeed, she has no experience to help build her self-efficacy for playing any style of guitar with other people. Therefore, a teacher should address this lack of experience. One easy fix is for them to practice as a duo during lessons.

The teacher in our example has used vicarious experience to help build his student's self-efficacy for rock music by showing her examples of female rock guitarists, but he needs a novel strategy for this new motivation challenge. He recalls that another student told him that playing duets with him helped her feel more comfortable playing with others, so he starts there. He picks a few songs that he thinks she will be

Implications for Motivating Others 65

able to learn quickly and will enjoy playing. Then, they learn to play the songs together. He uses this new experience of mastery to try to help her see that playing with others is a new challenge that can be fun. The important point in this case is that he wants her to have and recognize a concrete mastery experience playing with him, as that will help her build her self-efficacy for playing with others. As Dale Schunk's research has suggested, we often need to point out successes to students and help them own those experiences before they will increase their self-efficacy.[45,46,47] This is where persuasion can work hand in hand with past mastery experiences to encourage positive self-efficacy.[4,5,29]

Often when a teacher, friend, parent, or coach wants to encourage someone's motivation, it is because s/he believes the student will enjoy and/or be successful at the task. We become concerned when we think someone will not try, or not try hard enough, due to lack of information or a negative impression that is holding him/her back. The person who wants to motivate another person needs to frame the process of trying in terms that are meaningful to the student (friend, child, etc.). Helping the student see the relevance to a meaningful future goal can be a powerful way to complement the effort to encourage self-efficacy. We need to be careful, however, to find the goal that resonates with the student. Teachers and parents are quick to use college and/or future employment as future goals, but these may be too distant or just not relevant to the student's present concerns. Rather, we need to understand the future goals that the student is striving for before we can help the student see how the current work relates to that meaningful future goal.

For example, when a middle school student is at risk for being held back in the seventh grade, the salient future goal

Implications for Motivating Others

might be moving to the eighth grade so that s/he can enjoy being with friends in classes. We can also remind the student that, following a school failure, s/he will lose eligibility to play a sport that the student enjoys. Those two goals might be more salient and motivating than progress toward college or other post-secondary goals. Importantly, we want to heed the research of Vansteenkiste et al. and Tabachnick et al., which I mentioned in Chapter 4, by promoting the intrinsic or personally meaningful aspect of the future.[43,44]

For the guitar student, the future goal aspect is straightforward because she has already experienced some enjoyment of the new genre. The teacher has that intrinsic part of the future goal readily at hand. He could augment it with stories of adults who are happier and less stressed when they continue a hobby such as guitar playing, but her future enjoyment should be the first goal that he encourages. He needs to remind her that playing with others will develop her skill and offer a new avenue for enjoyment of that skill.

Now let us return to Jenice, who is learning algebra for the first time, to see how self-efficacy and future goals might help her to maintain her motivation. This example is useful for several reasons. First, self-efficacy is likely to suffer during school-based transitions,[25] probably due to the newness of the situation overshadowing past mastery experiences. Also, when students first encounter algebra, it is not uncommon for them to fail to recognize it initially as mathematics that they are prepared to engage. As noted previously, Jenice is likely going to need help, in the form of persuasion from the teacher and/or parent, connecting her past mastery to this new class before she feels self-efficacious. Importantly, though, she is also going to need to experience success in the new class. Persuasion based on past mastery in math is not going to be as

Implications for Motivating Others 67

strong as actual mastery with the new material. That is why practice with feedback is so important when people are learning new skills. In classes like algebra, all students need ample opportunities to experience mastery of a new form of mathematics if they are to develop positive self-efficacy.

Dale Schunk and his colleagues conducted quite a bit of relevant research on how to promote self-efficacy.[45,46,47,48] This research examined different facets of self-efficacy development and found several key outcomes. First, their findings support the role of attributions. Attributions refer to the reasons people cite for successes and failures. Attributions fall within the interpretive aspect of motivation that I have been referencing throughout this book, which reminds us how significantly the individual's perception of past experiences, persuasive arguments, role models, and physiological responses matters. We want to help people internalize their successes such that they see themselves as agents of their successes. In Schunk's work with middle school students with learning difficulties, he found that helping students develop positive attributions for success enhanced their self-efficacy.[47] He also found it helpful to use peers as models, especially when the student perceived the model as being similar, and when the model experienced failure or challenge and coped with that experience.[46,47] In other words, watching someone experience challenge, recover, and move on was a vicarious experience that actually helped students with their own self-efficacy. Related to my next example, Schunk also found that, when encouraging students' self-efficacy, using a combination of rewards and students' own goals for success was most powerful.[46]

We have talked about Jenice in terms of how we might provide support for her self-efficacy. Now I want to explore the issues of motivating her with future goals. This is a fairly typical but complex case. We do not have much knowledge of Jenice's distant future goals; we only know that her mother is employed in a field linked to mathematics (engineering). We do not want to assume that Jenice will be going into a similar field, so we may want to focus on her keeping her options open. For many college-bound students, being reminded of the role of mathematics can be crucial for them getting into their college and major of choice. We also would talk to her about how getting the first algebra class out of the way early will allow her more choices for her future math and science classes. This might appeal to her wish to take courses of interest later on in high school. We would encourage her to think about how she might enjoy having that flexibility in high school. We want her to think that mastering this class will lead to something meaningful in the not-too-distant future. This example shows us that it is not always straightforward or easy to find that link from the present to the desired future. However, for most students there will be something—even if it is not as concrete as future acceptance into an architecture program or pre-medical studies.

CLASSROOM EXAMPLES

I focused first on individuals rather than classrooms because teachers are often involved in the motivation of individuals in their classrooms on top of their normal classroom practices for positive motivation. Teachers create an overall classroom environment that can be motivating or discouraging, but they also reach out to individual students who they identify as needing one-on-one encouragement. Teachers who are successful in motivating their students learn how to both create the overall positive environment for students and identify ways to encourage individual students. I will present examples and ideas for elementary and secondary classrooms to discuss how self-efficacy and future goals can be encouraged at the classroom level.

Before I move on to specific examples for elementary and secondary classrooms, I want to point out two research-supported practices that are important for all teachers seeking to encourage positive motivation (and I will reiterate these in the final chapter). First, students need to experience success, which means that teachers need to recognize when otherwise effective instruction is not working for some of their students. Teachers should have plans for those students who do not succeed with the main lesson. Having a good idea of where students are starting from with their knowledge is necessary to planning effective instruction. That brings me to the second practice needed. Teachers need a working knowledge of their students' background knowledge, skills, interests, and aspirations. This can be tricky for secondary teachers in charge of large class sizes. We should examine how these practices might work somewhat differently for elementary and secondary teachers.

Elementary Classrooms

Let's return to our example of the fifth-grade teacher who loves teaching science. In this school, he teaches all subjects so he must be careful to show enthusiasm for all his lessons. This can be a noteworthy challenge. Anyone who has taught a class knows that teachers are not uniformly motivated to teach all the content in their classes or at particular grade levels. The elementary teacher who teaches all subjects must prevent his/her differences in motivation from affecting students. Students construct their knowledge and their motivation based on the learning context (including the teacher), their background knowledge and experiences, and their interpretations of the learning context.[35] However, the elementary teacher has the power to structure the educational experience of his/her students in ways that relay powerful messages about the fun or utility of any subject. When subtle messages indicate, for example, that topics in social studies are boring and less useful than science, students may internalize the messages over the course of the school year. This social studies example came to mind largely because I recently saw a young journalist quizzing other young people about basic US history. Many of the young people being quizzed did not know who won the US Civil War or from what country the United States became independent! These same young people, however, were fluent in celebrity culture. My point is that the elementary teacher who teaches all subjects must encourage positive motivation for all the subjects even though s/he will not always have such positive motivation within him/herself.

It is important to note that it is not just a matter of teachers demonstrating their own motivation. Instead, teachers should learn how to introduce new lessons with multiple reasons for why they are important, making multiple pitches for the relevance of the new material. Future goals are important here because, in most cases, some students will not be moved by pitches that focus on intrinsic motivation or fun. Teachers should always try to make new materials sound intriguing and the lesson fun, but with the knowledge that that pitch will not resonate with all students. We need to recognize that external reasons will resonate with many students, but their efforts will not be geared toward deep understanding. These can be reasonable short-term goals, but unless there is more internalization of reasons for doing the work, the student will likely not learn well enough for the material to be useful

Implications for Motivating Others 71

when it is needed in the next unit or grade level.[1,42,43] Extrinsic goals are fine for students starting from amotivation, but they will not sustain motivation or encourage deep learning over time.

Supporting Future Goals in the Elementary Classroom

When it comes to pitching future goals, our fifth-grade teacher needs to consider what is relevant to his students. Convincing students that they will be able to use information outside of school can be meaningful to them—particularly elementary-age students, for whom an appeal to their increased autonomy and growing sophistication can resonate. For example, students with younger siblings might be motivated to read stories to those siblings. The ability to make change and shop on one's own can be motivation for learning math. The ability to talk to adult family members about current issues can be motivating for learning social studies. School-minded students can be reminded of the ways that the current lesson will prepare them for upcoming material. Ongoing success in school is probably a good pitch to make even for those students who have not yet registered the importance. Planting the seed that success in learning begets future success in learning is important for all students.

To sum up my recommendation about pitching future goals, a major point is that we teachers should engage in ongoing reminders of why our classroom activities are important to students. We usually mention these issues at the beginning of a school year, but students need to be encouraged to think about what lessons mean to them so that they will engage in ways that help them learn. This is true of all levels and subjects of teaching, but at the elementary level it is especially important because we are trying to set students

72 Implications for Motivating Others

up for ongoing success in school. Their motivation for school will be key to that success.

Supporting Self-Efficacy in the Elementary Classroom

To enhance self-efficacy in the classroom, elementary teachers first need to accurately assess where students are starting from when new lessons begin. We want to build on their knowledge foundations. At the beginning of the school year, we need to figure out which of our students will likely need more help initially, and then we need to monitor all students throughout the year as they engage with new materials. If students struggle for too long with new learning, their frustration will lower their self-efficacy, which will discourage their ongoing efforts with similar tasks.

There are a couple of important points to consider when we talk about monitoring for frustration. First, appropriate levels of challenge are needed for motivation, rather than baby steps. Evidence tells us that humans grow, learn, and are motivated when faced with moderate challenge.[33] As I noted in Chapter 3, learning that is too easy becomes boring quickly and does not make students feel efficacious. Of course, when the challenge is too high, students become frustrated unless we help them through the challenge. The concept of instructional scaffolding is useful here. Oftentimes we want students to stretch their skills and knowledge with our new lessons, thus there is challenge built into the lesson. We should also build in different supports, such as hints and strategies, to help them accomplish this mental stretching. In educational psychology, we call these intentional hints and strategies instructional scaffolds. They are planned ways of providing the support students need to engage with tasks of moderate challenge. We can also use other students to provide scaffolding, or one-on-one support when a student is frustrated by a new lesson. Sometimes help from another student will be more powerful than help from the teacher because another student is a more similar model for encouraging self-efficacy. As many teachers know, this type of pairing in class can offset the boredom of the student who moves quickly with certain assignments, as well as help the student who needs further attention.

The use of novelty in lessons follows the same pattern as does challenge. Novelty often increases the initial interest in engaging in a lesson, which is always good, but novelty can also backfire if confusion ensues. Novelty and challenge can go hand in hand, and therefore both should be used with scaffolds in mind. Scaffolds can provide the necessary support for self-efficacy, so that the challenge and novelty are enjoyable. Scaffolds can also be built into the fun aspect of a lesson. For example, giving students hints can make the lesson seem more like a game or puzzle. In fact, we can use the analogy of games to think about how supporting self-efficacy can also support ongoing motivation. Games have challenge and leveling up (which is simply learning how to play the game better), but if we do not experience success early on, we quickly lose interest in the game. Students who enjoy digital gaming often discover hints or "cheats" that help them master the game. These cheats are the scaffolds. Another aspect of games that relates to self-efficacy is the constant provision of feedback about one's progress.

Our fifth-grade teacher who loves teaching science has likely learned how to develop science lessons that are challenging and include novelty. While science education historically promotes more discovery-based lessons than other areas, elementary education as taught to preservice teachers has generally moved toward more discovery- or constructivist-based instructional methods over expository (or teacher-led) instruction. However, with more discovery-based approaches, the need for instructional scaffolds also becomes greater for supporting student self-efficacy. Teachers sometimes forget that challenge and novelty, while supportive to initial engagement in lessons, can quickly lead to disengagement when self-efficacy begins to falter. Our fifth-grade teacher also will need to check that his own enthusiasm for his science lessons will not impede him from monitoring the ongoing motivation of his students. Sometimes we cannot fathom why others do not enjoy what we enjoy, and this can make it more difficult to notice that others are not as motivated as we are. The bottom line is that teachers need to be intentional when monitoring their students' self-efficacy and possible needs for further instructional support.

Another way this fifth-grade teacher should be intentional is while using his motivation for teaching science to plan similarly motivating lessons for the other subjects. For him, the features of science lessons that encourage initial and ongoing motivation can provide a template for figuring out the elements that would facilitate engaging lessons across subjects. For example, many of the discovery techniques that work in science can be replicated in mathematics. In teaching mathematics, elementary teachers sometimes revert to drilling skills because they do not recognize that the same learning and motivation principles apply to learning new mathematical concepts. There are still benefits to using traditional math exercises, but they should probably follow from the initial concepts that students can learn through discovery-based activities. Please note that I am not making the case for all-discovery instruction or all-constructivist teaching.[49] There

Implications for Motivating Others

are sound reasons for using expository lessons and skill-and-drill practice, but good teaching involves thoughtful and effective use of all techniques.

We noted earlier in the book (see Chapter 3) that students need informational feedback to develop self-efficacy. Elementary teachers need to build feedback into their lesson planning so that students receive accurate information about their progress. Sometimes we also need to interpret the feedback for students. Remember that students who are struggling with their self-efficacy might not recognize when feedback tells them they are mastering the material. When a class finishes a particularly challenging lesson, teachers might want to take a moment to note such success to make sure that students are owning their progress and not attributing it to excessive teacher assistance. Reminding students of their role in their own learning and progress will help them develop positive self-efficacy.

Secondary Classrooms

The challenges for teachers motivating secondary students are different in some ways. On the one hand, many students bear a developed stance toward school, especially by the ninth grade. On the other hand, successful transition to post-secondary adulthood can be a powerful future goal for many, if not most, students. Sadly, though, there is evidence that motivation to learn generally declines from elementary to secondary.[50,51] However, research has also identified nuances related to who is going to experience declines and why, and these findings can help us identify strategies for interrupting the decline.[52,53,54] There are two key findings that I would like to highlight. First, declines begin with decreasing self-efficacy. When students lose confidence in their abilities in domains, such as literacy and math, declines in their overall motivation for those domains follow.[52] Second, research has shown that secondary schools that emphasize democratic practices (i.e., more choice and autonomy for students and greater focus on mastery over competition) tend to minimize declines in motivation.[53,54] I will use these two general findings to frame my recommendations for secondary classrooms.

Supporting Self-Efficacy in the Secondary Classroom

There are some specific issues that secondary teachers should consider in addition to the recommendations noted for elementary teachers. Older students are more concerned with privacy surrounding their failures and doubts about their efficacy than elementary-aged students, and they have greater needs for autonomy and control. When secondary students fail and/or show signs of lower self-efficacy, teachers need to prioritize more individualized outreach. They need to put students in the position of planning for and controlling the process of recovery from failure. If a teacher perceives the problem to be beyond his/her content area, then the school counselor or psychologist can better work with the student. Teachers should still offer options for one-on-one help or recommend outside tutoring, as they would with younger students, particularly for students who have fallen behind in class or started the class with insufficient background knowledge and skills. However, the teacher should be more diligent about privacy concerning students' needs for these options.

In addition to their needs for greater privacy surrounding self-efficacy struggles, secondary students also need more opportunities to be autonomous. The process of making choices and learning from the consequences of those choices is important for developing positive self-efficacy. Here is where differences between school subjects become important to consider. With language arts and social studies, we can easily see how choice can be incorporated into the curriculum within classes. Students can be encouraged to follow their interests when choosing books and projects to explore. This might also be true in science classes, to the extent that students are assigned independent projects. In mathematics, the choices are more often between classes rather than within classes. This varies across school districts to some extent, but often students can choose how far they move toward college-level mathematics. In the science curriculum, students also encounter more between-class choices. These between-class choices can have far-reaching consequences, so students should be counseled regarding those consequences. When we provide students with choices within their classes, they are likely to be better prepared for the between-class choices.

I was involved in a series of studies in a high school computer programming class that effectively demonstrates how choice can encourage or discourage motivation, and the role of teacher support in this process.[55,56] In both studies, we introduced a discovery-based project into a largely teacher-led programming class. We asked high school students to use an online game to develop instruction for fifth-grade students. In the first study, we saw that students initially devised highly ambitious project ideas that were beyond their level of expertise and beyond what the teacher could scaffold in the time allotted (which was two weeks). Their self-efficacy plummeted when they realized that they could not complete these ambitious projects. The students, who were initially very motivated for this novel project, became discouraged and then reverted to ideas that were simple and would probably be boring for the fifth-grade class. In a subsequent iteration of the study, we introduced a similar project, but we provided more scaffolding up front, along with actual feedback from fifth-grade students. In the first study, the students did not have enough expertise to make good choices about the project. In the second study, we supported their self-efficacy by scaffolding their choices of projects to develop before integrating authentic feedback, via the fifth-grade "clients," that allowed them to continue or modify the initial project. The result was that most students engaged with an interesting project that they were ultimately able to complete. Challenge and novelty were involved in both cases, but without scaffolding and feedback, one group's self-efficacy faltered and group members' projects suffered.

Another strategy that secondary teachers can consider is the use of cooperative learning to help students develop and maintain positive motivation. Cooperative learning has been studied for many years, and we know that learning groups work best when the groups are heterogeneous in their makeup (students bring different knowledge, skills, and personalities) and when there is both individual accountability and a group reward.[57] Individual accountability means that each person in the group earns his/her own grade on the assignment. That helps offset what I call the "slacker effect," whereby some students let others do the bulk of the group's work. It also encourages self-regulation because students need to figure out how the group work will allow them to achieve their personal goals. A group reward—that is, an incentive for the group to work together—can inspire cooperation and collaboration. The group reward also encourages a focus on each participant, since the reward is given only when everyone in the group does well. Teachers often give bonus points or some other recognition when the whole group performs well. Of course, cooperative learning groups can be used at all levels of education, but it is important here to note that they are quite useful at the secondary level for promoting motivation and learning.

There are studies that have shown that cooperative groups lead to more positive motivation, including higher self-efficacy.[58,59] Both of the theories I presented in Chapter 2 can be used to understand why there might be positive effects of cooperative learning on motivation. From Social Cognitive Theory, the structure of cooperative learning allows students to observe how other students perceive learning, think about and reason with the specific task, and express their motivation to learn. From Self-Determination Theory, cooperative learning overtly supports the need for relatedness and can also support competence and autonomy.

Supporting Future Goals in the Secondary Classroom

Post-secondary adulthood is a major future goal that secondary teachers can utilize for motivating their students, especially at the high school level. Secondary teachers need to figure out how their students expect to spend their initial years out of high school, and use that for motivation. However, adults often make the mistake of using these goals in a threatening way, which is not going to be motivating in the long run. As the evidence that I have cited so far suggests, getting students to focus on intrinsically meaningful goals is most productive.[43,44]

When helping students think about how schooling might be instrumental for their post-secondary goals, teachers should realize that what seems obvious to a teacher or parent is not often obvious to the student. Students often need instruction and/or mentoring to break down a long-term goal into subgoals. This can be accomplished in all grade levels across domains. Secondary students, especially through the ninth grade, do not always innately know how to break a large project down into smaller pieces. The same problem is likely true with their out-of-school goals. Therefore, when we introduce large projects that we expect students to work on over time, we can talk about how the project could or should be broken down and how that process is similar to how we approach projects outside of school. This may help students learn how to be more proactive in their academic and out-of-school lives. This process should be discussed in classes and then modeled for students. Teachers can talk about how they plan for a big family vacation, for example. I talk to my students about how I plan for grading during the busy evaluation periods of the semester. Given that my students are pre-service teachers, this discussion is relevant to them for several reasons. I want them to know that getting timely feedback to them is a meaningful goal for me, but often still a tedious task given the volume of work that I must grade. I tell them that rewarding myself for meeting my subgoals (finishing some number of papers or exams) can help me complete the larger goal of completing all the grading. Nearly every teacher has some personal self-regulation technique that can be shared in order to model the process for his/her students.

I would also like to point out here that, obviously, not all secondary students are going to be motivated by post-secondary goals. Middle school students have more short-term concerns that we need to use for motivation. Sometimes that means talking to them about the goal of advancing to a new grade level rather than repeating the current one. As with elementary teachers, secondary teachers need to know what their students care about so that those concerns and goals can be

Implications for Motivating Others

used in positive ways to encourage them to learn material that will be relevant in the future.

CONCLUSION

The purpose of this chapter was to present scenarios and recommendations that allow us to think about the implications of self-efficacy and future goals. We looked at our guitar student and our young algebra learner as examples. By focusing on these two examples, I have shown that understanding the individual's perceptions and concerns is central to encouraging his or her motivation. I also detailed recommendations for both elementary and secondary classrooms. Given the unique characteristics of children and adolescents, it is difficult to scale motivation interventions up to the classroom level.[33] Indeed, we are challenged to motivate ourselves, not to mention our students. However, as teachers, parents, friends, etc., we often find ourselves wanting to help someone overcome a motivation problem with concrete strategies. Many of the ideas we have for motivating individuals can be tried at the classroom level. Indeed, there are some common ideas that permeate the research on how to enhance motivation to learn. Teachers should learn about their students' short- and long-term goals and focus on mastery and meaning when planning lessons and when talking to students about reasons for learning.

Six

Conclusions

In this final chapter, I will present some cautionary comments about oversimplifying constructs that have important nuances. I will also describe where I think the research should be going in order to maximize the impact that teachers and parents can have on self-efficacy and future goals. I will close with some final thoughts on motivating others.

The purpose of this book has been to clarify and simplify, to some extent, two important concepts related to motivation to learn in order to demonstrate their accessibility beyond the academic literature. The reader should, though, know that there are hundreds of academic papers on self-efficacy alone and fewer, but still many, on how the future can shape present motivation. This volume of research literature speaks to the complexity and importance of the two concepts. I would love to be able to claim that it is easy to use these concepts to motivate others, but anyone who has tried to reason with a seemingly unmotivated person knows the challenges of making an impact. Nonetheless, these two concepts provide foundations for our persuasive efforts. Plus, the research is clear that addressing issues of self-efficacy and future goals will be more effective for ongoing motivation than bribing people with financial or material rewards. That is not to say that most of us will never attempt to bribe a student at some point when they have mentally "checked out," but SDT tells

Conclusions 83

us that we need to nudge such students toward more internalized regulation once we have gotten them trying to learn or minimally engaging in learning and/or studying.

One factor that limits our ability to use self-efficacy and future goals to motivate people to learn is that the available research has largely avoided substantive coverage of the racial/ethnic issues surrounding self-efficacy and future goals. Although there are some studies that focus on race, very few studies on motivation and race are published in educational psychology journals, from which I have drawn the research base presented here.[60] As DeCuir-Gunby and Schutz addressed in a recent article, our field needs to engage in more research that examines constructs like self-efficacy and future goals with race-focused and race-reimaged approaches.[60] Issues of race and cultural differences need to be at the forefront of the research on motivation rather than relegated to secondary or control variables. This will require researchers to think differently about samples, measurements, and methodologies for their work. One good example of research in this vein is a recent study on self-efficacy from Ellen Usher's P20 Motivation and Learning Lab.[61]

This type of culturally relevant future research will allow us to examine the extent to which our theories extend to non-majority cultures. Additionally, we will have more information about how to persuade students of color to be sufficiently motivated for school success. First, though, educational psychologists need to learn how to focus on social structures rather than exclusively individual, psychological constructs.[60] This may require collaborations with educational policy makers and sociologists who know how to study the macro issues that influence student motivation.

There has been a greater volume of research on gender differences and motivation. One interesting finding from our

84 Conclusions

work on motivation for high school mathematics was that the retention of stereotypes about the importance of math learning for boys at the expense of girls resulted in both male and female students exerting less effort to learn mathematics.[20] We speculated that the underlying reasons for the shared negative relationship were different, but the main take away is the same: Mathematics education should hold equal relevance to the futures of both male and female high school students. Indeed, classrooms that proceed as such have reported increases in self-regulated learning. We also reviewed research on gender differences and the role of future strivings.[19] That review of research indicated that both males and females had developed similar post-secondary goals, but how they visualized the timing of the goals was different. This suggests that we need to understand the nuances of future strivings when we intervene to help students become more motivated or maintain their positive motivations.

Another area for future research will be on how to scale up from interventions that focus on individuals or small groups of students to classrooms and/or schools. As Urdan and Turner noted, this type of research is difficult to conduct for a host of reasons.[33] For one, we are not sure if the typical findings represent aspects of classrooms that teachers can implement with consistency and fidelity. One clear finding is that teachers should attempt to provide optimal challenges in the tasks that they have their students perform. It is difficult to assess and provide optimal challenges across 20 to 125 students, however. Nasir and Hand noted that it is easy to lose site of the larger structural issues when trying to shift teaching or classroom practices toward race-sensitive interventions.[62] Nonetheless, as educators, we would like to see more attempts at classroom- and school-level interventions. We also hope those attempts will include ways to address the diversity of student motivational needs. Research has shown that high school classrooms that facilitate and support mastery experiences, interesting and relevant tasks, and student autonomy are predictive of higher self-efficacy and future goals.[39] These findings should be applied to intervention research, despite the many challenges.

CONCLUSIONS

My hope is that I have convinced the reader that the concepts of self-efficacy and future goals are both understandable and important. The major limitation comes with the dearth of research detailing larger-scale interventions. On the one hand, we know that the concepts of self-efficacy and future goals are very personal and meaningful at the level of the individual; on the other hand, knowing what teachers might do to improve motivation at the level of the classroom can only come from further research in this area. In the meantime, we have learned something about how we can persuade individuals to be more motivated. Most of us have been in the position of wanting to help a friend, student, or child overcome a motivational challenge, and these two concepts will prove vital to these situations.

To encourage positive self-efficacy, we first and foremost must allow students to experience success. For a student with a history of failure, tutoring or intense practice might be needed before the motivation angle can or should be tackled. Next, we need to persuade students to see their successes as due to their own agency. We need to remember that students who struggle with motivation sometimes attribute their successes to luck or help from others.[46] Part of the struggle is to recognize their own agency when success happens. As

Conclusions

Schunk's work has demonstrated, students can be persuaded with effective peer modeling to internalize their successes.[48] We need to remember that transitions, such as those between tasks, classes, and schools, are central points during which self-efficacy is likely to flag and require support.[33]

Future goals are perhaps the most overlooked and/or poorly used tool for motivating others. They are a good choice for persuasion when you know that the person does not yet experience intrinsic motivation. The trick—for teachers and parents—is to determine what future goals would be meaningful to the person and then show him/her how the current learning challenge is instrumental to those future goals. We can encourage people to strive toward meaningful goals and help them learn strategies that will make their strivings more successful. As Schunk found, helping students to recognize their goals and learn new strategies for success also helps them develop positive self-efficacy.[46,47]

Glossary

Amotivation When a student shows no attempts to learn the material for any reason.

Basic needs Theory and research lend support to the idea that humans have needs for competence, autonomy, and relatedness.

Big theory A theory that has multiple components and is designed to explain a lot of related phenomena.

Extrinsic motivation When a student has goals for doing schoolwork that are reasons other than enjoyment of mastering the material. These goals can be understood as existing on a continuum from completely external (as when the only reason is obtaining some reward outside of the learning—such as grades and money for grades) to more internalized (as when the learning is important to the individual's sense of self). On the more internalized end of the continuum, learning is not enjoyable, but it is still meaningful. The more internalized, according to Self-Determination Theory, the more self-regulated the student will be in his/her attempts to learn.

Future goals Goals for the future that help people see that the current context is instrumental for obtaining that desired future. For example,

	if the future goal is to be a dentist, then doing well in school now is important to that future goal. These are extrinsic goals that have been internalized such that they are personally meaningful.
Instructional scaffolding	Intentional hints and strategies in lessons that are provided to help students work through the initial challenges in a lesson. For example, in a math exercise in which students need to solve for area, remind them that they know the relevant formulas and should have those formulas ready to use.
Instrumentality	The quality whereby something is useful to something else. For example, good health is instrumental to a long, productive life.
Mastery experience	An experience in which success was achieved. These experiences can be used to build ongoing motivation.
Perceived instrumentality	Recognizing that something is useful for obtaining something else. When the future goal is being a dentist, success in school is central to obtaining that goal.
Self-concept of ability	How we think and feel about ourselves in regards to domains or subjects such as mathematics and athletics.
Self-Determination Theory (SDT)	A big theory that holds that human well-being is largely based on one's sense of control over his/her life. The satisfaction of basic needs and the distinction between intrinsic and extrinsic motivation are central components.
Self-efficacy	A person's belief about whether s/he is capable of successfully completing a given task.

Self-regulated learning	Active, thoughtful pursuit of desired learning goals through planning, enacting, monitoring, controlling, and reflecting upon internal (i.e., cognition, metacognition, motivation, behavior, affect) and external factors (i.e., environment) before, during, and after learning.
Self-regulation	Active planning, enacting, monitoring, control, and evaluation of cognition, affect, motivation, and behavior in the pursuit of valued goals, particularly when encountering impediments to that pursuit; in this text, this term is used to describe the pursuit of goals aside from those related to learning academic material.
Social Cognitive Theory (SCT)	A big theory of learning that focuses on how human action is based on the self-system responding to internal and external information. Learning through observation is one key element.
Vicarious experience	When we witness the successes and failures of others. Depending on how similar the other is to us, we might be able to derive self-efficacy information from the other's experience.

References

1. Ryan, R. M., and Deci, E. L. (2000). Self-determination theory and the facilitation of intrinsic motivation, social development, and well-being. *American Psychologist*, 55, 68–78.
2. Covington, M. V. (2000). Intrinsic versus extrinsic motivation in schools: A reconciliation. *Current Directions in Psychological Science*, 9(1), 22–25.
3. Stipek, D. J. (1996). Motivation and instruction. In D. C. Berliner and R. C. Calfee (Eds.), *Handbook of educational psychology*, 1st Edition (pp. 85–113). New York: Macmillan Library Reference.
4. Bandura, A. (1977). Self-efficacy: Toward a unifying theory of behavioral change. *Psychological Review*, 84, 191–215. Retrieved from http://doi.org/10.1037/0033-295X.84.2.191
5. Gottfried, A. E., Fleming, J. S., and Gottfried, A. W. (2001). Continuity of academic intrinsic motivation from childhood through late adolescence: A longitudinal study. *Journal of Educational Psychology*, 93, 3–13.
6. Bandura, A. (1986). *Social foundations of thought and action: A social-cognitive theory*. Englewood Cliffs, NJ: Prentice Hall.
7. Wertheimer, M. (1979). *A brief history of psychology*. Revised Edition. New York: Holt, Rinehart & Winston.
8. Anderson, J. R. (2010). *Cognitive psychology and its implications*. 7th Edition. New York: Worth.
9. Greene, J. A. (2018). *Self-regulation in education*. New York: Routledge.
10. Greene, B. A. (2015). Measuring cognitive engagement with self-report scales: Reflections from over 20 years of research. *Educational Psychologist*, 50(1), 14–30, doi:10.1080/00461520.2014.989230
11. Deci, E. L., and Ryan, R. M. (1985). *Intrinsic motivation and self-determination in human behavior*. New York: Plenum.

References

12. Miller, R. B., Greene, B. A., Montalvo, G. P., Ravindran, B., and Nichols, J. D. (1996). Engagement in academic work: The role of learning goals, future consequences, pleasing others and perceived ability. *Contemporary Educational Psychology*, 21, 388–422.
13. Miller, R. B., DeBacker, T. K., and Greene, B. A. (1999). Future goals and academics: The link to task valuing. *Journal of Instructional Psychology*, 26, 250–260.
14. Gjesme, T. (1979). Future time orientation as a function of achievement motives, ability, delay of gratification, and sex. *The Journal of Psychology*, 101, 173–188.
15. Gjesme, T. (1981). Some factors influencing perceived goal distance in time: A preliminary check. *Perception and Motor Skills*, 53, 175–182.
16. DeVolder, M. L., and Lens, W. (1982). Academic achievement and future time perspective as a cognitive-motivational concept. *Journal of Personality and Social Psychology*, 42, 566–571.
17. Nuttin, J. (1985). *Future time perspective and motivation: Theory and research method*. Hillsdale, NJ: Erlbaum.
18. Husman, J., and Lens, W. (1999). The role of the future in student motivation. *Educational Psychologist*, 34, 113–125.
19. Greene, B. A., and DeBacker, T. K. (2004). Gender and orientations toward the future: Links to motivation. *Educational Psychology Review*, 16, 91–120.
20. Greene, B. A., DeBacker, T. K., Ravindran, B., and Krows, A. J. (1999). Goals, values, and beliefs as predictors of achievement and effort in high school mathematics classes. *Sex Roles*, 40(5), 421–458.
21. Eccles, J. S., and Wigfield, A. (1995). In the mind of the actor: The structure of adolescents' achievement task values and expectancy-related beliefs. *Personality and Social Psychology Bulletin*, 21(3), 215–225.
22. Reeve, J. (2006). Teachers as facilitators: What autonomy supportive teachers do and why their students benefit. *The Elementary School Journal*, 106, 225–236.
23. Bong, M., and Clark, R. E. (1999). Comparison between self-concept and self-efficacy in academic motivation research. *Educational Psychologist*, 34(3), 139–153.
24. Bong, M., Cho, C., Ahn, H. S., and Kim, H. J. (2012). Comparison of self-beliefs for predicting student motivation and achievement. *Journal*

of *Educational Research*, 105(5), 336–352. Retrieved from http://dx.doi.org.ezproxy.lib.ou.edu/10.1080/00220671.2011.627401

25. Schunk, D. H., and Pajares, F. (2005). Competence perceptions and academic functioning. In A. J. Elliot and C. S. Dweek (Eds.), *Handbook of competence and motivation* (pp. 85–104). New York: Guilford.

26. Baumeister, R. F., Campbell, J. D., Krueger, J. I., and Vohs, K. D. (2003). Does high self-esteem cause better performance, interpersonal success, happiness, or healthier lifestyles? *Psychological Science in the Public Interest*, 4, 1–44.

27. Baumeister, R. F., Campbell, J. D., Krueger, J. I., and Vohs, K. D. (2005). Exploding the self-esteem myth. *Scientific American*, 292, 84–91.

28. Forsyth, D. R., Lawrence, N. K., Burnette, J. L., and Baumeister, R. F. (2007). Attempting to improve the academic performance of struggling college students by bolstering their self-esteem: An intervention that backfired. *Journal of Social and Clinical Psychology*, 26(4), 447–459.

29. Zimmerman, B. A. (2000). Self-efficacy: An essential motive to learn. *Contemporary Educational Psychology*, 25, 82–91.

30. Marsh, H. W., Roche, L. A., Pajares, F., and Miller, D. (1997). Item-specific efficacy judgments in mathematical problem solving: The downside of standing too close to trees in a forest. *Contemporary Educational Psychology*, 22, 363–377.

31. Schunk, D. H., and Mullen, C. A. (2012). Self-efficacy as an engaged learner. In S. L. Christenson, A. L. Reschly, and C. Wylie (Eds.), *Handbook of research on student engagement* (pp. 219–235). New York: Springer.

32. Hong, Y., Chiu, C., Dweck, C. S., Lin, D. M., and Wan, W. (1999). Implicit theories, attributions, and coping: A meaning system approach. *Journal of Personality and Social Psychology*, 77(3), 588–599. Retrieved from http://search.proquest.com/docview/614335906?accountid=12964

33. Urdan, T., and Turner, J. C. (2005). Competence motivation in the classroom. In A. J. Elliot and C. S. Dweck (Eds.), *Handbook of competence and motivation* (pp. 297–317). New York: Guilford.

34. Tomlinson, C. A. (2014). *Differentiated classroom: Responding to the needs of all learners*. Alexandria, VA: Association for Supervision & Curriculum Development.

35. Maehr, M. L. (1984). Meaning and motivation: Toward a theory of personal investment. In C. Ames and R. Ames (Eds.), *Research on motivation*

in education: Student motivation (vol. 1, pp. 115–144). New York: Academic Press.
36. Pintrich, P. R. (2000). An achievement goal theory perspective on issues in motivation terminology, theory, and research. *Contemporary Educational Psychology*, 25, 92–104. doi:10.1006/ceps.1999.1017
37. Anderman, E. M., and Patrick, H. (2012). Achievement goal theory, conceptualization of ability/intelligence, and classroom climate. In S. L. Christenson, A. L. Reschly, and C. Wylie (Eds.), *The handbook of research on student engagement* (pp. 173–191). New York: Springer.
38. Smith, M., Duda, J., Allen, J., and Hall, H. (2002). Contemporary measures of approach and avoidance goal orientations: Similarities and differences. *British Journal of Educational Psychology*, 72(2), 182.
39. Greene, B. A., Miller, R. B., Crowson, H. M., Duke, B. L., and Akey, C. L. (2004). Predicting high school students' cognitive engagement and achievement: Contributions of classroom perceptions and motivation. *Contemporary Educational Psychology*, 29, 462–482.
40. Malka, A., and Covington, M. V. (2005). Perceiving school performance as instrumental to future goal attainment: Effects on graded performance. *Contemporary Educational Psychology*, 30(1), 60–80.
41. Miller, R. B., and Brickman, S. J. (2004). A model of future-oriented motivation and self-regulation. *Educational Psychology Review*, 16, 9–33.
42. Husman, J., Derryberry, W. P., Crowson, H. M., and Lomax, R. (2004). Instrumentality, task value, and intrinsic motivation: Making sense of their independent interdependence. *Contemporary Educational Psychology*, 29(1), 63–76. Retrieved from http://search.proquest.com/docview/620296883?accountid=12964
43. Vansteenkiste, M., Lens, W., and Deci, E. L. (2006) Intrinsic versus extrinsic goal contents in self-determination theory: Another look at the quality of academic motivation. *Educational Psychologist*, 41, 19–31.
44. Tabachnick, S. E., Miller, R. B., and Relyea, G. E. (2008). The relationships among students' future-oriented goals and subgoals, perceived task instrumentality, and task-oriented self-regulation strategies in an academic environment. *Journal of Educational Psychology*, 100(3), 629–642.
45. Schunk, D. H., and Pajares, F. (2002). The development of academic self-efficacy. In A. Wigfield and J. Eccles (Eds.), *Development of achievement motivation* (pp. 15–31). San Diego, CA: Academic Press.

References

Retrieved from doi:http://dx.doi.org.ezproxy.lib.ou.edu/10.1016/B978-012750053-9/50003-6

46. Schunk, D. H. (1984). Enhancing self-efficacy and achievement through rewards and goals: Motivational and informational effects. *Journal of Educational Research*, 78, 29–34.
47. Schunk, D. H., and Cox, P. D. (1986). Strategy training and attributional feedback with learning disabled students. *Journal of Educational Psychology*, 78(3), 201–209.
48. Schunk, D. H., and Hanson, A. R. (1989). Influence of peer-model attributes on children's beliefs and learning. *Journal of Educational Psychology*, 81(3), 431–434.
49. Kirschner, P. A., Sweller, J., and Clark, R. E. (2006). Why minimal guidance during instruction does not work: An analysis of the failure of constructivist, discovery, problem-based, experiential, and inquiry-based teaching. *Educational Psychologist*, 41(2), 75–86.
50. Anderman, E. M., and Maehr, M. L. (1994). Motivation and schooling in the middle grades. *Review of Educational Research*, 64(2), 287–309.
51. Eccles, J. S., and Roeser, R. W. (2011). Schools as developmental contexts during adolescence. *Journal of Research on Adolescence*, 21(1), 225–241.
52. Archambault, I., Eccles, J. S., and Vida, M. N. (2010). Ability self-concepts and subjective value in literacy: Joint trajectories from grades 1 through 12. *Journal of Educational Psychology*, 102(4), 804.
53. Vedder-Weiss, D., and Fortus, D. (2011). Adolescents' declining motivation to learn science: Inevitable or not? *Journal of Research in Science Teaching*, 48(2), 199–216.
54. Vedder-Weiss, D., and Fortus, D. (2012). Adolescents' declining motivation to learn science: A follow-up study. *Journal of Research in Science Teaching*, 49(9), 1057–1095.
55. Ge, X., Thomas, M. K., and Greene, B. A. (2006). Technology-rich ethnography for examining the transition to authentic problem-solving in a high school computer programming class. *Journal of Educational Computing Research*, 34, 319–352.
56. Thomas, M. K., Ge, X., and Greene, B. A. (2011). Fostering 21st century skill development by engaging students in authentic game design projects in a high school computer programming class. *Journal of Educational Computing Research*, 44, 391–408.

References

57. Slavin, R. E. (1996). Research on cooperative learning and achievement: What we know, what we need to know. *Contemporary Educational Psychology*, 21(1), 43–69.
58. Thoonen, E. E. J., Sleegers, P. J. C., Peetsma, T. T. D., and Oort, F. J. (2011). Can teachers motivate students to learn? *Educational Studies*, 37(3), 345–360. Retrieved from http://search.proquest.com.ezproxy.lib.ou.edu/docview/871543166?accountid=12964
59. Krause, U., Stark, R., and Mandl, H. (2009). The effects of cooperative learning and feedback on e-learning in statistics. *Learning and Instruction*, 19(2), 158–170. Retrieved from http://search.proquest.com.ezproxy.lib.ou.edu/docview/621811307?accountid=12964
60. DeCuir-Gunby, J. T., and Schutz, P. A. (2014). Researching race within educational psychology contexts. *Educational Psychologist*, 49(4), 244–260. doi:10.1080/00461520.2014.957828
61. Ahn, H. S., Usher, E. L., Butz, A. R., and Bong, M. (2016). Cultural differences in the understanding of modelling and feedback as sources of self-efficacy information. *British Journal of Educational Psychology*, 86(1), 112–136. doi:10.1111/bjep.12093
62. Nasir, N. S., and Hand, V. M. (2006). Exploring sociocultural perspectives on race, culture, and learning. *Review of Educational Research*, 76, 449–475. doi:10.3102/00346543076004449

Index

Note: Page numbers in *italics* denote references to figures and tables.

academic achievement 34, 37–8
accountability, individual 78
achievement goals 52–3
all-constructivist teaching 74
amotivation 71
attributions 67
autonomy 22, 28–9, 45, 47, 76–7

Bandura, A. 40
Baumeister, R. 44
behaviorism 12–14
behavior modification plans 20
Bong, Mimi 35, 36
Brickman, S. J. 57

Clark, R. E. 35
classroom bucks 29–30, 33
cognitive revolution 12
competence 22, 29
competence domains 34
competition 46
complex learning 5–6
contextual cues, shaping people's behavior 12–13
cooperative learning 78–9

Deci, E. L. 21, 59
DeCuir-Gunby, J. T. 83
differentiated instruction 43–5
diminished motivation 41
discovery-based education 73–4
distant future goals 57

elementary classroom 69–75
engagement 31, 51, 53, 62, 63, 74
environmental cues 14
Expectancy-Value Theory 27, 58–9
external incentives 56–7
external rewards 29–30
extrinsic goals 54, 71
extrinsic incentives 56
extrinsic motivation: intrinsic vs. 2–4, 21; for ongoing motivation 22; rewards and punishments 2–3; schools operating in 30; *see also* motivation; rewards and punishments
extrinsic utility values 58–9
extrinsic valuing 58–9

feedback to students 7; Controlling versus informational 29, 45–6, 47
Forsyth, D. R. 37
future goals: in the classroom 61; current behaviors linking to 51; definition of 1, 50; in elementary classroom 71–2; gender differences in 83–4; instrumentality and 56–60; intrinsic 59–60, 66; mastery goals vs. 53–6; outcome expectations 55–6; perceived instrumentality 57–8; performance approach 52–3; performance avoidance

52; predicting effort and achievement 59; predicting self-regulation 59; racial/ethnic issues 83; relating current work to 65–6; in secondary classrooms 79–81; in self-determination framework 53; subgoal strategy 79–80; task-specific 50–1; task values vs. 59
future time orientation 26–7
future time perspective 26–7

gender differences 83–4
global self-esteem 36–8
group reward 78–9
guilt, avoiding 25, 26

Hand, V. M. 84
Handbook on Competence and Motivation (Urdan and Turner) 43

incentives for student participation 29–30, 33; *see also* extrinsic motivation; intrinsic motivation
informational feedback 45–6, 75
instructional scaffolding 72–3, 77–8
instrumentality 56–60
internalization process 25–6
internalized meaning 3, 25
intrinsic motivation: classroom environment supporting 7–8; external rewards as hindrance to 29–30; extrinsic vs. 2–4; future goals and 59–60; for guitar 4–6; as internalized form of motivation 3; for mathematics 6; *see also* motivation; rewards and punishments
introjected regulation 24, 25

learning motivation: physical space 18; social environment for 19–20
Lens, W. 59

manipulation, by incentives 33
mastery experiences: classroom implications 43–4; creating 65; as evidence to support self-efficacy 5; recognizing past 40, 48, 66; setting students up for 47
mastery goals 52–6
Miller, R. B. 57
moderate challenge 7, 29, 35, 44, 47, 72
motivation: challenges to 80–1; diminished 41; elementary classrooms 69–75; examples with individuals 64–8; extrinsic incentives in 56; extrinsic vs. intrinsic 2–4; inference of others 63; race and 83; in secondary classrooms 75–6; student diversity and 84–5; undermining 4; *see also* extrinsic motivation; intrinsic motivation; rewards and punishments

Nasir, N. S. 84
negative outcome expectations 55–6
novelty in lessons, use of 73–4, 78

observation 63
outcome expectations 55–6
out-of-school goals 80

peer competition 46; *see also* persuasion by others
peer modeling 20, 67, 86
perceived instrumentality 57–8, 60
performance approach goals 52–3
performance avoidance goals 52
persuasion by others 40, 42, 48, 65–7; *see also* peer competition
physiological responses to experiences 42–3, 49
positive motivation 29
punishments *see* rewards and punishments

racial/ethnic issues 83
reasons goals 50
Reeve, Johnmarshall 28
reflective activities 19–20
relatedness 22, 29
relaxation 43
rewards and punishments: classroom bucks 29–30, 33; as extrinsic motivation 2–3; group reward 78–9; as hindrance to intrinsic motivation 29–30; reinforcement of 12; *see also* motivation
role models 41, 49, 67, 86
Ryan, R. M. 21

Schunk, Dale 65, 67, 85–6
Schutz, P. A. 83
secondary classroom 75–81
self-beliefs, hierarchy of 34–8
self-concept of ability 34–5
Self-Determination Theory: autonomy and 22; classroom implications of 28–30; competence and 22; cooperative learning and 79; definition of 9, 21; extrinsic motivation and 21; gradations of external and internal motivation 22–3; intrinsic motivation and 21–2; motivation types and associated regulatory styles 23–5, 24; relatedness and 22; understanding future goals with 31
self-efficacy: in the classroom 47; classroom implications 43–8; definition of 1, 35, 39–40, 48; developing 31, 40–3; in elementary classroom 72–5; focusing on cognitive appraisals 35–6; generality of 38–9; physiological responses and 42–3; predictive power 39; promoting 67; racial/ethnic issues 83; in secondary classrooms 76–9; support for 43–4; vicarious experience and 41–2
self-esteem 34, 36–8
self-esteem programming 37
self-perceptions 34
self-regulation: component skills of 16; definition of 15; future goals and 51; future goals predicting 59; personal techniques 80; regulatory styles 23, 24, 27;
situational information 17–18
slacker effect 78
Social Cognitive Theory: behaviorism and 12–13; for the classroom 17–21; cooperative learning and 79; definition of 9, 11; human agency and 13; self-regulation and 15–16; situational information 17–18; student behavior and 17–20; triadic reciprocality 13–14; understanding learning and motivation 20–1
social environment 19–21
social learning 15, 41, 46; *see also* vicarious experience
social persuasion 42, 48
students: autonomy of 45, 47, 76–7, 85; experiencing success 69; focusing on own work 46–8; participation incentives 29–30, 33; privacy concerns 76; relating current work to future goals 65–6; sense of competence 45
subgoal strategy 79–80
sustained effort 4–6
symbolic processing 14

Tabachnick, S. E. 62
task-specific goals 50–1
teachers: acknowledging student's feelings 29; autonomy-supporting 28–9; challenging students 84;

Index

classroom activities, importance of 71–2; classroom environment supporting 18–19; demonstrating own motivation 70; developing assessments of students' knowledge 44; differentiated instruction and 43–5; encouraging intrinsic motivation 7–8; instructional scaffolding 72–3; motivating secondary students 75–6; providing student feedback 45; supporting positive self-efficacy 43–4; of tightly controlled classrooms 45; use of novelty in lessons 73–4

theories: behaviorism 12–14; benefits of 10; Expectation-Value Theory 27; testing 10–11; *see also* Self-Determination Theory; Social Cognitive Theory
triadic reciprocality 13–14
Turner, J. C. 43, 84

Urdan, T. 43, 84
Usher, E. 83

Vansteenkiste, M. 59, 62
vicarious encouragement 17
vicarious experience 15, 41–2, 48, 64

For Product Safety Concerns and Information please contact our EU
representative GPSR@taylorandfrancis.com
Taylor & Francis Verlag GmbH, Kaufingerstraße 24, 80331 München, Germany

www.ingramcontent.com/pod-product-compliance
Lightning Source LLC
Chambersburg PA
CBHW052027290426
44112CB00014B/2417